Intercultural
DESIGN
BASICS

Advancing Cultural and
Social Awareness through Design

by Susanne P. Radtke

BI**SPUBLISHERS**

Written by Susanne P. Radtke
www.intercultural-design-basics.com

Typeset in TheSans and TheMix
provided by LucasFonts

BIS Publishers
Borneostraat 80-A
1094 CP Amsterdam
The Netherlands
T +31 (0)20 515 02 30
bis@bispublishers.com
www.bispublishers.com

ISBN 978 90 6369 604 7

Copyright © 2021 Susanne P. Radtke and BIS Publishers.

Layout: Susanne P. Radtke, Angela Ziegler
Specialized editing: Dr. Anni Peller
English translation: Lindsay Jane Munro

Acknowledgments
This book would not have been possible without the
valuable input and generous support I received from friends
and colleagues. These include: Nada Hussein Abdallah,
Rayan Abdullah, Lariset Aguilar, Engy Aly, Sigrid Bathke,
Benjamin Bayer, Ilona Bubeck, Margarita Budini, Jan Büttner,
Christa Casel, Ashley Cooper, Paul Daniel, Emel Eren,
Maria Garaeva, Cornelia Häusler, Zari Harat, Andi Haryanto,
Nawar Haytham, J. Ellen Hogue, Hanny Kardinata, Daniela
Kirchlechner, John Kudos, Henri Kusbiantoro, Huang Li, Zhiqian Li,
Jim Baker, Christina Lobenberg, Georgios D. Matthiopoulos,
Mirza Maulana, Lewis Nightingale, Jayesh Patil, Saskia Pferrer,
Golnar Kat Rahmani, Lars-Thore Rehbach, Stephan Saaltink,
Erich Schmidt-Dransfeld, Wolfgang Schwarz, Verena Seitz,
Mimi Sheiner, Mengxuan Sun, Heri Susila, Pilar van der Lugt,
Jamila Varawala and, of course, all of those who remain
unnamed here, but whose advice, insider knowledge and
contributions were invaluable.

My special thanks go to Elizabeth Resnick, who so kindly and
generously provided me with access to her international
network of designers, Lara Ledwa for her meticulous editing
and her important comments about political terminology,
Lindsay Jane Munro for her diligent translation, Angela Ziegler
for the attractive layout and her stamina, as well as Anni Peller
for her encouragement, for keeping me on track and for her
support in the academic research work, above all on the texts
on color semantics, Cuba and Poland.

User instructions
The book comes with a learning app that offers
hands-on, fun and interactive content!

Install the app in just 3 steps:
↗ Download the "Intercultural Design Basics" app from
the Google Play Store or Apple's App Store. As an owner
of the book, you will receive our app for free!
↗ Find your website access code on the label on the front flap.
Enter it on the following website:
www.intercultural-design-basics.com
You will then receive your personalized Play Store or
App Store promo code.
↗ Now unlock the app using your promo code.

Point the camera of your smartphone or tablet at the QR codes
in the book and off you go!

The following content is available on the app:

▶️ Videos (interviews with designers, workshops and animations)

🔲 Projections in augmented reality (visual input in 3D space)

🗔 Galleries and slideshows (learning – step by step)

🎮 Games (learning by doing)

Have fun!

CONTENT

FOREWORD

This publication is not only a textbook for teaching students of design and communication, but is also aimed at teachers of design, media and marketing. Together with the accompanying learning app, the book provides a global and innovative approach towards design education and training. A wide range of cultural insights are provided, and fundamental theories of design, typography, color and semiotics are introduced. Readers gain a clearer understanding of how these are applied in praxis thanks to the diverse international design works presented. These also serve to draw attention to international designs and styles that many readers may not yet be familiar with. An understanding and estimation of cultural diversity is an excellent foundation for successful intercultural communication. I go one step further in my intercultural workshops, demonstrating how intercultural competence can be initiated and encouraged.

This book deliberately gives space to the different perspectives, experiences and pedagogical approaches of international designers and design educators. It aims to explore very complex topics in visual communication in the international context, so that intercultural and innovative learning contents can be expanded upon.

The first chapter examines the meaning of the form of signs and sign systems, which are always embedded within a cultural context and can only be understood and interpreted via this context. They are important for designers in understanding how communication functions – both in theory and in practice.

The second chapter looks at the fundamental elements and forms of visual communication like the point, line and plane, exploring our visual perception in terms of size, brightness and contrast. It also examines in more detail culturally and individually shaped habits in how we look at things and our need as human beings for balance and stability.

The third chapter presents type and type systems. Beginning with a definition and brief history of how character codes developed, this chapter goes on to explain the cognitive processes of reading, type anatomy, type classification and legibility. International designers and their typographic work are presented and discussed in order to clarify cultural contexts and provide different meanings and interpretations.

Color, which is one of the most important elements in graphic design, is the focus of the fourth chapter. We perceive of color in a myriad of different ways that are highly influenced by our cultural environment. It is important that students of graphic design are aware of the different associations invoked by colors and color combinations. This chapter also highlights and explains culturally different color design using a number of international design works.

Chapter five takes a closer look at how design works in praxis. Design is strongly linked to socio-cultural aspects, and so this chapter presents design workshops in which the participants are of different nationalities. Methods, processes, topics and experiences from these workshops are presented, with a particular focus on how working together in internationally mixed teams influences the resulting design work of the students.

The sixth and last chapter follows on from this to show how, in a globalized world, design maintains its local character. This is a phenomenon that globally operating companies pay heed to in their advertising. Taking the three countries Cuba, Poland and Indonesia as examples, this chapter sheds light on the historical developments that led to the current forms of graphic design in each of these three nations.

SIGNS

Complex sign systems already emerged thousands of years ago in China and in Mesopotamia, a part of the Near East, to name only two cultures. Modern semiotics, which is the study of sign systems, is a relatively young discipline. It goes back to antiquity and is important for understanding design and modern communications.

In the Middle Ages, scholars answered the question concerning what a sign was with *aliquid stat pro aliquo,* that is: the one stands for the other. Accordingly, a sign has a representative function, it can materialize in a concrete form. It can, for example, be carved into stone, like a Greek or Roman statue of a God that represents certain properties.

Right up to the present day, the statue of Justitia stands for (state) justice and her three attributes - the blindfold over her eyes, the scales and the executioner's sword - are supposed to express that the court is unbiased, and that it weighs matters in a balanced manner and that it judges in a just manner. Justitia is not a real person, just like the pop-culture heroes Superman and Batman, who create their own areas of law enforcement. Superheroes are brands that have fan items and also logos, of course.

Architecture also transmits messages by acting – already visible from the distance – as distinctive features or landmarks of a place. The Eiffel Tower stands for Paris, the Golden Gate Bridge for San Francisco and the distinctive Opera House stands for Sydney.

Our entire cultural world and our perception of it are penetrated through and through with signs. Everywhere we look, our world is full of countless signs, for example, traffic signs, phonetic symbols, hand signals, smoke signals, company signs and letters, to name but a few.

1.01 World of signs
1.02 Justitia, personification of justice
1.03 Background photo: Australia, cave painting

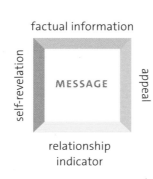

factual information

MESSAGE

self-revelation

appeal

relationship
indicator

SENDER
with 4 mouths

RECEIVER
with 4 ears

1.04 Communication
square according to
Schulz von Thun

The communication square

Signs serve first and foremost to communicate, to exchange information. At the end of the sixties, the communication theorist and philosopher Paul Watzlawick, working in a research team in California's Palo Alto, formulated five axioms to explain human communication. The most well-known of these five axioms states that we cannot not communicate. What that means, is that we are always transmitting non-verbal messages through our behavior, even when we are silent.

A follow-up model with a strong practical component was developed at the beginning of the 1980s by psychologist Friedemann Schulz von Thun. This model is used a great deal in communication courses, and according to the model, every message has four different facets.

We all know the situation where we are trying to communicate something, but our listener does not understand what we are trying to say (or cannot or does not want to understand). Our message might be very clearly and unequivocally formulated, and yet we don't get the intended message across. Why is that the case? Because there is no such thing as purely factual information. Every statement we make is imbued with our personal feelings, whether we are aware of that or not.

This is also the case in professional life, for example, at a lecture on a specific subject. We aim to address our listeners in the best way possible with an interesting topic, the factual information. We pay attention to how we come across on a personal level and to what we reveal of ourselves. That is the self-revelation. By going into contributions to the discussion, we show that we respect our vis-à-vis thus giving a relation-

"One cannot not communicate."

Paul Watzlawick

ship indicator. We focus on what it is we want to achieve in our listener. This part of the message contains an appeal.

How our listeners interpret our messages and how they see us as a person does not have to coincide with our intentions. Clarifying this discrepancy and improving the exchange of information is the declared aim of all communication models.

The sender-receiver model

As human communication is so complex and multi-layered, it is worth examining the sender-receiver problem first of all by looking at a much simpler technical system for transmitting signals, namely the early 20th century telephone. When the sender-receiver model became popular, the devices used to transmit and receive messages were mainly landline telephones and cable connections that transmitted electrical signals.

In the 1940s, the mathematician Claude E. Shannon and the communications engineer Warren Weaver were commissioned by a telephone company with reducing the susceptibility to disruptions in the transmission of signals. They developed the so-called Shannon-Weaver Model.

For the purpose of understanding, let's first look at how acoustic signals are transmitted

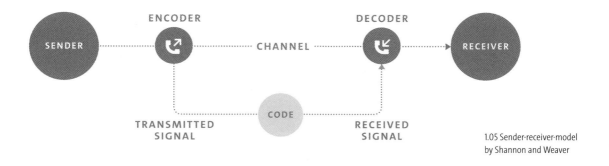

1.05 Sender-receiver-model
by Shannon and Weaver

when we communicate with one another without a transmission device. We use our voice to communicate a piece of information, meaning our thoughts are transformed into sounds and words, that is, into acoustic signals. The sound waves are transmitted through the air to the ear of the receiver, transformed into neuronal signals, i.e. they are decoded, so that we can hear the spoken word; unless there is a disruption of some kind, for example loud music.

When we, as the sender, use a telephone as the transmitting device, information is converted, i.e. encoded, into electrical signals via the microphone in the form of sound waves. The signals are sent via a channel (electric cable or radio) to the loudspeaker of the receiving device and decoded there so that they arrive with the receiver in the form of sound waves. During this process, disruptions like back-

ground noise can occur. The sender-receiver model can also be applied to the communication between computers. This clearly structured sender-receiver model was adapted by many other disciplines, for example, the social and communication sciences, and it was expanded to include psychosocial and marketing-relevant aspects. However, a technical model does not deal either with the person of the sender or the receiver, or with the content of the communication. That is why the model is only transferable to a limited extent.

As such, the term 'disruption' has negative connotations in the technical context, whereas in education and intercultural communication, a 'disruption' can actually be helpful or important. A disruption in the flow of communication can help one to identify cultural differences or to reflect on what one is saying.

INTERPRETANT

SIGN

OBJECT

1.06 Semiotic triangle

SOUND-IMAGE

Signifier
(le signifiant)   [dɔːg]

- -

CONTENT

Signified
(le signifié)

1.07 Model of signs by Ferdinand de Saussure

**The triangle of reference /
semiotic triangle**

In philosophy, the examination of signs
went down a very different path. In the
19th century, the linguist Ferdinand de
Saussure developed semiology (as a part
of semiotics) to become an important
branch of epistemology. He defined the
sign as a unit made up of sound-image
(expression) and concept (meaning, concept). The communicating sign, e.g. the
sound [dɔːg] is referred to as the signifier
(le signifiant). The communicated content,
the fact that it is about a dog, is referred
to as the signified (le signifié). In this dyad-
ic (consisting of two elements) sign model,
the object, i.e. the dog to which the sound
[dɔːg] refers, plays no role yet.

A contemporary of Saussure, the American philosopher Charles Sanders Peirce, developed a sign model that was based on the triad object – sign – interpretant. The linguists Charles Kay Ogden and Ivor Armstrong Richards later coined the term semiotic triangle.

The object refers to the actual content being communicated. The sign shows how one represents or names it; it therefore has a presence that can be perceived of by the senses. The sign might be a pictogram of a dog, like the sign used to instruct people to keep their dog on a leash, but it could also be barking that alludes to a dog.

What the sign means is described by the interpretant (signifier/referent). If we, for example, hear a dog barking, we form a term, an idea. Someone who is afraid of dogs will imagine something different from someone who loves dogs. As one of the founders of American Pragmatism, Peirce sees the creation of signs (semiosis) and their meaning as an effect-oriented process that includes us as the users of signs.

1.08 "Wau Wau", card game by Mimi Rehmann

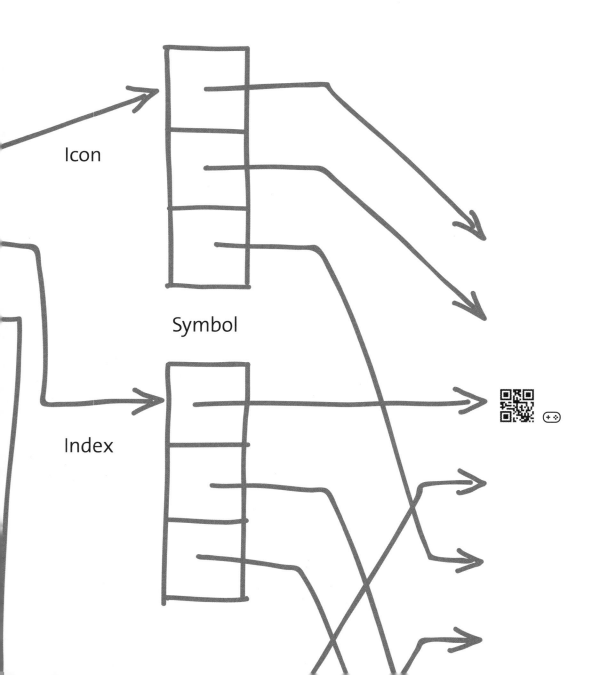

Icon

Symbol

Index

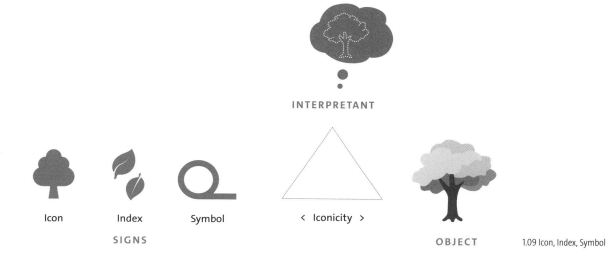

INTERPRETANT

Icon   Index   Symbol   < Iconicity >

SIGNS   OBJECT   1.09 Icon, Index, Symbol

Relevant for design practice are Peirce's three categories of the sign or the bearer of the sign: icon – index – symbol.

Let us look at the object "tree". The iconic sign counterpart would be every image that is similar to the tree as an object: a true-to-detail illustration or also a pictogram-like image of the tree.

The indexical sign refers to an actually existing object. It has a factual connection, but no similarity to the object. Leaves lying on the ground allude to trees, but they do not look like trees. An index is a sign that bears a temporal and a spatial relationship to its object or referent. A classic example is smoke, that stands for fire, or a fingerprint, which alludes to a specific person. Indices can also be symptoms like fever for illness.

The symbol refers to the object as the result of a rule or convention. Most symbols are based on an "unspoken" and culturally conditioned concurrence. The relationship is both conventional and arbitrary. The sign used on maps to refer to trees is a symbol that first has to be learned. Other symbols are traffic signs, religious symbols, logos, symbols used in the natural sciences and letters of the alphabet.

There is a subdivision in icon, the iconicity, which describes the similarity to the object. The degree of iconicity is reduced to the extent that the degree of abstraction of the image increases. The more abstract the image of the tree, the lower the iconicity. The abstraction process plays a considerable role in design in an increasingly complex world, as simplifying processes and efficient orientation are essential in the real and digital world.

The abstraction process

The London Tube map is an example that has cult status among cartographers, as the technical draughtsman Harry Beck did away with the topographically authentic illustration in favor of a schematic one. He focussed on the essential elements like stations and line intersections and standardised the lines into horizontals, verticals and diagonals at 45° angles. This ground-breaking route map was introduced in 1933 and set a standard that influenced all such maps that followed.

At the beginning of the 20th century, minimalistic illustrations of nature were also preferred and, proceeding from Impressionism via Expressionism to Constructivism, the way was paved from figuration to abstraction. Piet Mondrian, together with Wassily Kandinsky, is among the founders of abstract painting, whereby Mondrian went the way of geometric abstraction, freeing himself gradually from the figura-

tive. Instead, Kandinsky wanted to express individual and spiritual experience, but later on as a Bauhaus lecturer developed a set of rules for his language of form that was universal.

There is basically no applied design without abstraction, as a message must be clear and unequivocal so that it can be decoded as free from disruption as possible by the receiver: think back to the Shannon-Weaver Model. But, unlike in art, design products are always directed at a use or an act.

↗ Focus on the essential elements
↗ Reduce the amount of elements

1.10 Logo development of "Pelikan", pen manufacturer

1938   2003

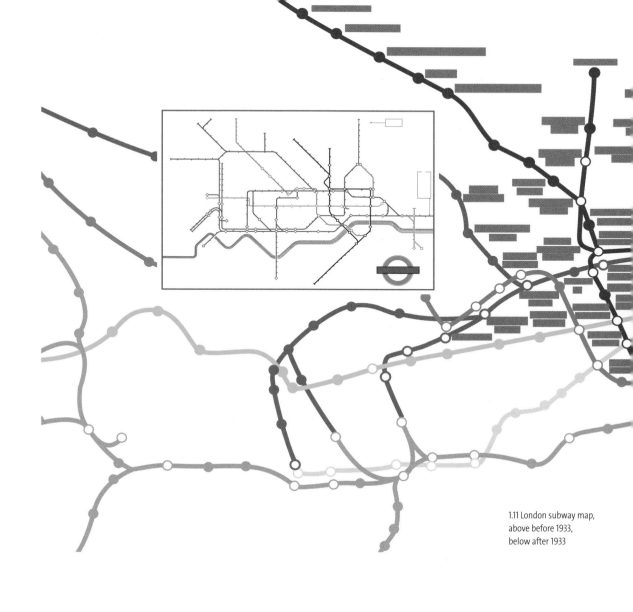

1.11 London subway map,
above before 1933,
below after 1933

1.12 Piet Mondrian,
Blossoming apple tree, 1912 /
Composition No. 11, 1913 /
Composition 1920

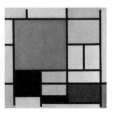

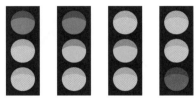

1.13 Semantics

Red: meaning is internationally consistent

Red-yellow: only applied in a few countries e.g.
Germany, Great Britain, Norway, Austria, Russia, Sweden,
Switzerland

Yellow, green: meaning is internationally consistent

Syntax–semantics–pragmatics

A contemporary of Peirce, the American philosopher Charles William Morris, pursued even more rigorously an application-oriented approach. Morris distinguished between the following three dimensions of the sign:

↗ Syntax (formal set of rules for a system of signs)
↗ Semantics (sign meaning)
↗ Pragmatics (sign use)

This categorization has established itself in all design disciplines, as it provides argumentation aids for practical design work.

Let's imagine we find ourselves on the street, standing in front of a traffic light. What do we see? First of all, three round surfaces in red, amber and green on a black background and, when the traffic light is in operation, these are displayed at different brightnesses. Circles are forms that, in this case, are the same size and arranged one below the other. They only differ in their color and have a high syntactic coherence, therefore a high formal connection. Under syntax, we understand forms, colors, brightness and

above all the relationship of the signs to one another.

The semantics describe the meaning, the content of the signs. The three signal colors red, amber and green mean: stop, wait and go. In addition, there are also color combinations that are displayed at the same time, like red-yellow, which means: attention, you can go very soon.

In the USA they also have a red flashing light which means stop but allows the driver to stop briefly and then continue on when the crossing is free of pedestrians. There are many differences and also different color combinations worldwide, but the color red always means stop and is always in the top position.

The pragmatics highlight the goal and the function of the sign. What act is it supposed to trigger? In our example, the car driver is supposed to stop at a red light, be ready to go at amber, and drive off at green. The detailed instructions for action are reflected in the traffic regulations, which are different worldwide.

We can only act appropriately in traffic when we know and can process all three sign dimensions, whether consciously or subconsciously. If we suffer from color-blindness, we may have problems with the syntax in certain circumstances, whereby the differences in brightness and the arrangement of the three circles help our perception.

Barrier-free signs are the tactile signal generators on traffic lights. They help people with impaired sight and the blind to negotiate traffic situations using orientation sounds and different vibration states.

1.14 Pedestrian lights, Germany

1.15 Pedestrian lights, f. l.t.r.: Guadeloupe, Germany, Denmark, Germany

1.16 Pedestrian lights, f. l.t.r.: Greece, Belgium, Netherlands, Austria

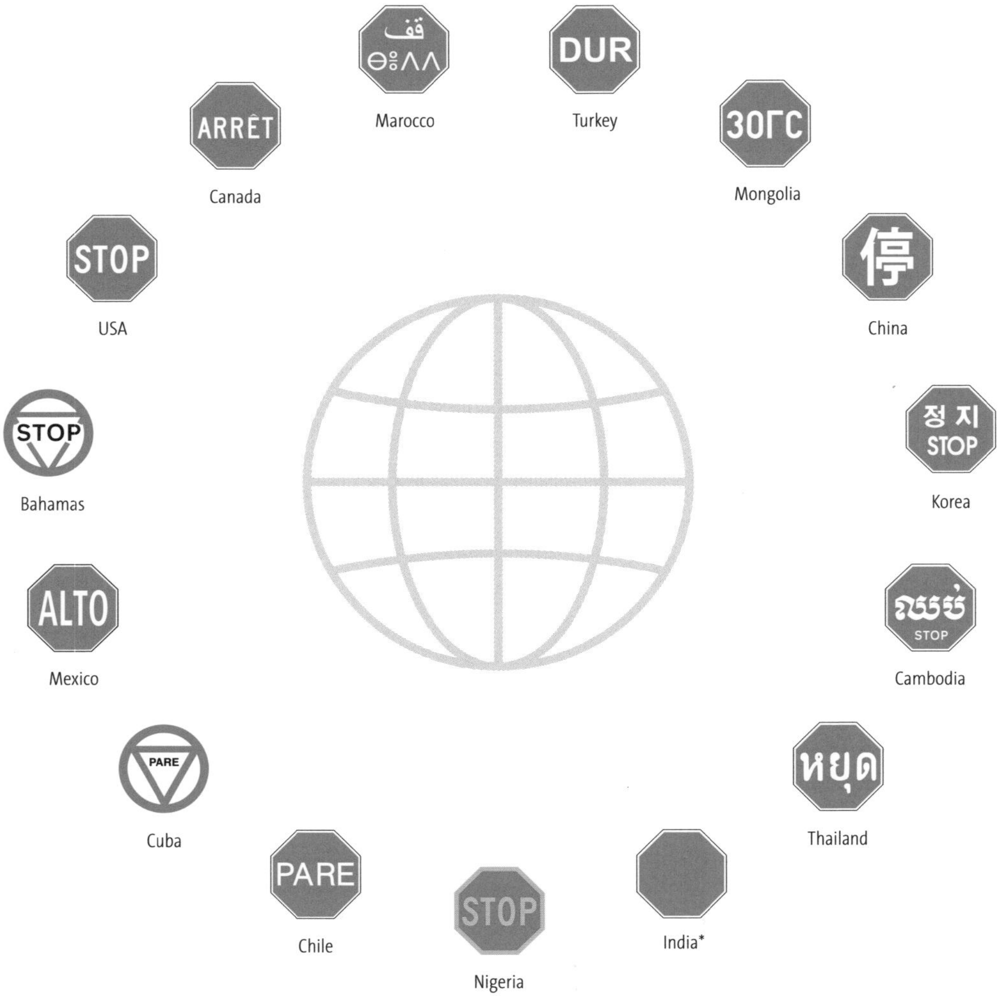

Marocco

Turkey

Mongolia

Canada

China

USA

Korea

Bahamas

Cambodia

Mexico

Thailand

Cuba

Chile

India*

Nigeria

* India has 23 official languages and over 100 other languages. Devanagari, Dravidian and Grantha are the main scripts, of which there are 13 in total. The stop sign is therefore displayed with a different font depending on the region, and there is also a version using "STOP".

London
1868

Italy
1896

USA
1924

Germany
1939

USA
1954

GDR
1956

Germany
1971

Japan

Papua-Neuguinea

Zimbabwe

Israel

1.17 International stop signs

International traffic signs
What exactly traffic signs mean is different internationally. When the encoding of the unfamiliar traffic sign is not known, its semantic dimensions cannot be understood at first glance.

It is helpful when important international traffic signs are understood by everyone participating in traffic. Writing and text should only play a subordinate role. The syntax of the international stop sign shows how important form and color are for identification/recognition purposes.

The red octagon, which was first introduced in the USA in 1955, has asserted itself worldwide. The international standardisation by the Vienna Convention on Road Signs and Signals from 1968 permits both the octagon and the circle.

RHOMBUS

Malaysia

Australia

Malaysia

Canada

Australia

USA

Indonesia

USA

Chile

Malaysia

TRIANGLE

Namibia

Spain-Tenerife

Germany

Swiss

Cuba

Russia

Israel

Sweden

Oman

South Africa

1.18 - 1.21 International traffic signs

CIRCLE

Australia

Indonesia

Italy

England

USA

Indonesia

Malaysia

New Zealand

Malaysia

China

SPECIAL TYPES OF SIGNS

Poland

Germany

Japan

Philippines

Australia

Colombia

Costa Rica

Syria

Italy

Colombia

Tradition ⟷ Pop culture

Tradition vs. pop culture

The historical sender-receiver model has served its time in Postmodernism, something that was expressed in the much-quoted sentence by Marshall McLuhan, *The medium is the message*. A handwritten letter carries content that is different from that in an SMS. SMS as a medium defines the content, the form, the transmission time and is not bound to a specific space. Luhan, a Canadian philosopher, already predicted in the 1960s the way that communication media would influence identity and society, at that time mainly radio and television. His vision of the future, the "global village", is a metaphor for the Internet today. His optimistic picture of a media society made him an icon of pop culture.

Pop culture is not the same as popular culture. Pop music is also not folk music, and the genre Pop Art has nothing to do with folk art, which is firmly anchored in history and in the manual crafts. Pop culture is everywhere: in comics, computer games, in visual art, films, advertising, merchandising products and in pop music. Its icons are real, like the Rolling Stones and the Spice Girls, but they are also hyper-real like Superman or Hello Kitty. What they all have in common is that they are products of the mass media and a globalized marketing strategy. Since the emergence of Postmodernism, that is, the era after Modernism, no difference is made in the media anymore between fiction and reality. Signs are no longer a reflection of reality, they are "hyper-real", i.e. they repress and replace reality.

This can be seen in the example of "Hello Kitty", the most famous Japanese Manga figure and a money magnet. The Kawaii cult figure *(kawaii*=cute) looks like a cat, even though the distributor Sanrio says it is supposed to be a London girl. The reference object is therefore a girl, the pictogram is a cat and the content is linked to the following message: "Hello Kitty represent the deep wish of every person, independent of nation and ethnicity, to experience happiness without judging this through a profound intellectual aspect." Hello Kitty is a mass media marketing and cultural product like Superwoman, Batman and Darth Vader, whose symbolic meaning is understood globally. Historically anchored symbols like the signs for Yin and Yang, the Wheel of Life and the Sphinx require explanation, unless they will be recycled by the media in future in a blockbuster or a series.

Hello Kitty
She represents Japanese pop culture and is omnipresent as a lifestyle brand – in fashion, cosmetics, toys, in food and beverages, the social media, etc.

Yin and Yang
In Chinese philosophy, polarities like cold and warm are not seen as opposites, but as a mutually defining unity.

Superman/Superwoman
Logo of the western comic heroes and founders of the genre. They share the same level of popularity as Batman and have a similarly high recognition factor.

Wheel of life
In both Hinduism and Buddhism, the Wheel of Life stands for the cycle of life from birth to death and to rebirth.

Batman
Batman does not have supernatural powers, but sophistication and toughness, and he is still a superhero thanks to his wealth and his intelligence.

Sphinx
A creature somewhere between human and animal that was widespread in Near Asia in antiquity and which still fascinates and puzzles us today.

Darth Vader
Warrior and antagonist in the science-fiction cult film Star Wars, which is one of the films that brings in most at the box office worldwide.

1.22 Poster "Stay home", 2020

1.23 Poster "Superhero doctors", 2020

Please describe your educational background, including your studies, work/study, and travel.

I was born in Israel and grew up in a crisis-torn region there, and experienced several wars in my youth, such as the Six-day War when I was ten years old. On the other hand, I was brought up in a household where it was very normal to fix things, as my father worked in construction. I was taught by my parents to make the world a better place. After I was in the military for 4 years, I traveled in the United States for a year. It was there that I discovered photography and its importance for me. I started to study Visual Communications in my twenties and graduated with a BFA when I was 26. I worked in several agencies before establishing my own agency in 2001. My political poster art developed parallel to that, as well as my comprehensive worldwide teaching.

Yossi Lemel
Studied at Bezalel Academy of Arts and Design, Jerusalem, Israel
Currently Senior Lecturer at Holon Institute of Technology, Israel
2001 Established Lemel Cohen Creative Factory, Tel Aviv Yafo, Israel

What countries or cultures have you worked with closely and/ or lived in? Have you had formative experiences in other cultures?

Communication – and language in particular – is a very important factor in my worldwide workshops. I communicate a lot with my students. I speak English, German, French and Hebrew and don't need a translator in most of the countries I teach in. But in some countries, such as Mexico, Turkey, Korea and others, students are not really fluent in English and I have to use translators. This is practical but makes the communication less direct and authentic, and only a part of the message is conveyed. My most formative experiences have been in Poland, as their visual culture – mainly in poster design – feels very close to my own art. It's almost as if the design there shares my own DNA.

What did you know about these countries/cultures before you started working together?

In my school days I was already exposed and influenced by late-seventies poster art from Poland; its Polish School of Poster Art. I was also influenced later in my design studies by the illustrator Seymour Chwast and his strong iconic visual language. As a designer, you have to be curious and to expand your horizons. Before I teach in another country with a culture that I don't know much about, I read as much as I can.

*What specific differences have you noticed in how students learn
in other countries/cultures?*

My approach to teaching and design is mainly conceptional and based
on the use of language. Therefore, the educational and communication
level is what makes the difference for me, not so much the culture.
German and Swedish students already have design skills, and their
English is mostly perfect, so I can easily get down to a content-based
depth. Not so in developing countries, where I have to deal with
the language barrier and often start at a different design level.

*Have you had to adapt your working or teaching methods while
exercising them in a foreign culture, i.e. adapting them to different
social and moral norms, including class or gender issues? If yes, how?*

I am very familiar with adapting culturally, as my parents migrated to
Israel as members of a Jewish community in Bedzin in Poland. They
had survived the Holocaust. My childhood in Israel was also marked
by intercultural and inter-religious themes.

It's important to me to see my students as individuals — not as for-
eigners — and to get to know them personally. I give them time and
space to talk about their lives and attitudes. I don't want to force my
ideas on them and I simply try to adapt to the given situation. I share
my comprehensive design and artwork with them and create space
for students' questions. I explain to them how I define problems
and how I combine ideas, concepts and words.

Teaching in countries that are politically unstable or that are some-
where between democracy and dictatorship can be a challenge.
In this case I cannot discuss everything I want to with the students.
In such cases, safety for the students and myself takes priority.

*What are the benefits you have gained from working in countries/
cultures that are different from your own culture?*

Teaching in other countries enriches your knowledge and widens
your horizons. You learn about the people, human conditions,
cultures. And also about differences in visual language, that means
color, typography, iconography and visual concepts. The more you
know about "the other", as it were, the more you understand it.

I create bridges and, for me, teaching feels like having a mission.
Being a teacher means exposing myself and often I am perceived
by students as a role model. That is quite a responsibility. However,
humor is an essential part of my teaching and I love wordplays
in any language.

1.24 Poster "Fake news", 2019

1.25 Poster "The Choice", 2020

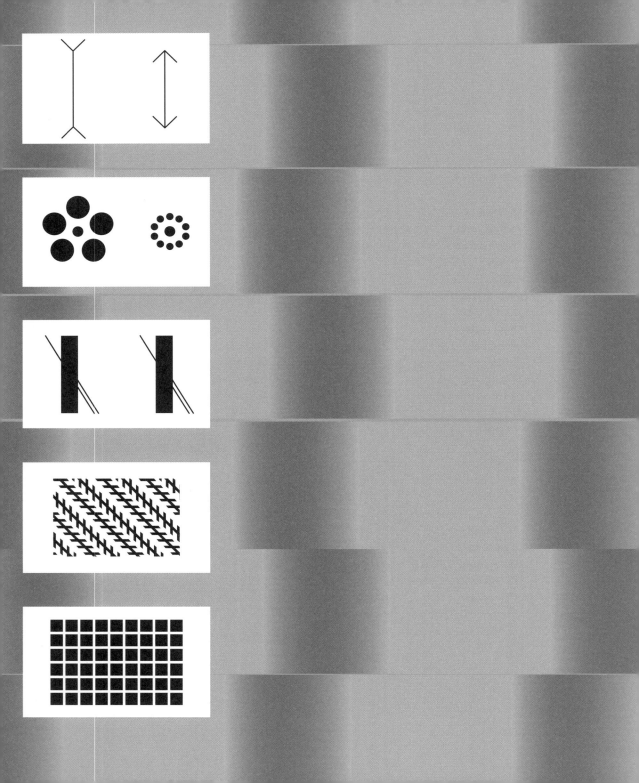

BASIC ELEMENTS AND BASIC FORMS

In general, we do not question our perception of things or the conclusions and emotions associated with these. How we perceive of things and what we perceive is however subjective and we can ultimately only communicate to others what a thing is like based on how we perceive it.

A tourist sees the strange environment in a different way to someone who is at home there. People in a wheelchair see high curbstones as an obstacle, while non-disabled people do not. All of us judge similar perceptions differently, depending on whether we are having a good day or a bad day, which is illustrated fittingly by the metaphor of the glass being half full or half empty.

Furthermore, the direction we read and write in also influences our preferred way of seeing things. If we primarily read from left to right, we prefer objects that face to the right; this is something that neuro-psychologists agree on. If we read and write from right to left, which is the case in Arabic, for example, depending on what study you read, objects facing left are preferred or both directions are judged without preference.

2.02 Preferred viewing direction when the direction you read and write in is from left to right

These are only a few examples of how differently our brains process visual information. And how little we can trust our senses is also shown by optical illusions, where size, brightness, contrasts and colors are not fixed constants.

However, when we strive to achieve professional skills of perception, because we want to work as a designer or to work creatively in the media, then it is vital that we train our perception. Having a knowledge of visual phenomena is only one side of the coin; the other side is getting to know and be aware of our individual preferences and perception habits. Only in this way can we have a common starting point from which we can then practice design in more depth.

2.01 A selection of optical illusions: 1. Müller-Lyer Illusion, 2. Ebbinghaus, 3. Poggendorff, 4. Zöllner, 5. Hermann-Gitter

The best way to train your own sense of perception is to use a setting that resembles an experiment in a laboratory: reduce things down to the essentials and eliminate all possible sources of interference with the aim of creating measurable and consistent behavior. First, we need a basic assumption. In this case, it is that basic emotional states such as harmony and disharmony are linked by most people – across cultures – to similar visual configurations.

In order to be able to judge a so-called figure on a surface, but also in space, we need another element: a frame or a ground. When we furnish our home, the size and proportions of the room play an important role, this is the so-called ground. A piece of furniture would then be the figure. If we reduce it to the bare essentials, a stool is initially all we need.

A stool, by the way, was also the first everyday object that former students at the Hochschule für Gestaltung Ulm, one of the schools that followed on from Bauhaus, had to make on their own in the wood workshop. It is known as the "Ulmer Hocker" (the Ulm stool). The stool was multifunctional and could be used both as a seat and, stacked on top of each other, as a standing desk or bookcase. This barren piece of furniture reflects the econo-mic restrictions of the post-war period as well as the will to make a fresh start. It becomes clear in many other places in this book, how important it is for the designer to be concerned with the simple and with the greatest possible clarity.

Let us imagine that we have a square surface area, which we call the ground, and a small black circular area as the figure. Where would we position it if we wanted to leave a harmonious impression on the onlooker? I have been conducting this experiment with students for more than 30 years, and I am still amazed after all this time at the conformity displayed in the outcome of this simple test. Try it yourself! Take a coin and position it within the square. The so-called figure-ground relationship should be as harmonious as possible.

The relationship between the ground and the figure is rarely balanced; it almost seems like a struggle to find the right balance. Many people have a need for stability. Just think what it feels like when we hang a picture and it is crooked at first. Designing has a lot to do with sounding out and balancing visual power relations. Gravity, which is known to us from physics, and the reading direction of Latin script have a significant influence on our viewing habits.

2.03 Position a coin inside the
square in such a way as
to achieve visual harmony.

Overview

↗ The point is the smallest element in design. Geometrically, it has no expanse and merely describes the position on a surface and in a space. In mathematics, the point is zero-dimensional.

↗ The line is made of many points and can be defined as the pathway of a moving point. The line always has a direction based on the reading direction and this lends it a dynamic quality. It has a length, but not a width. If you draw a line, then you create a boundary between two areas. Lines demarcate, separate and give order. They can be straight, curved or bent.

↗ The plane consists of rows of points. It has a size and a surface area that is defined by its width and length. We can only generate a figure-ground relationship and a positive-negative effect and create proportions using surfaces. The three basic forms square, circle and triangle are the bases for every other geometrical form.

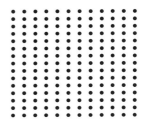

2.04 Design using basic elements

I BASIC ELEMENTS	II STATES	

THE POINT
Position: dimension 0

Symmetry, asymmetry, tension

Contrast, attraction/ balance, imbalance

THE LINE
Direction: dimension 1

Stability, instability, direction

Order, chaos, rhythm

THE PLANE
Proportion: dimension 2

Square, circle, triangle

Figure-ground relationship, proportion, positive-negative effect

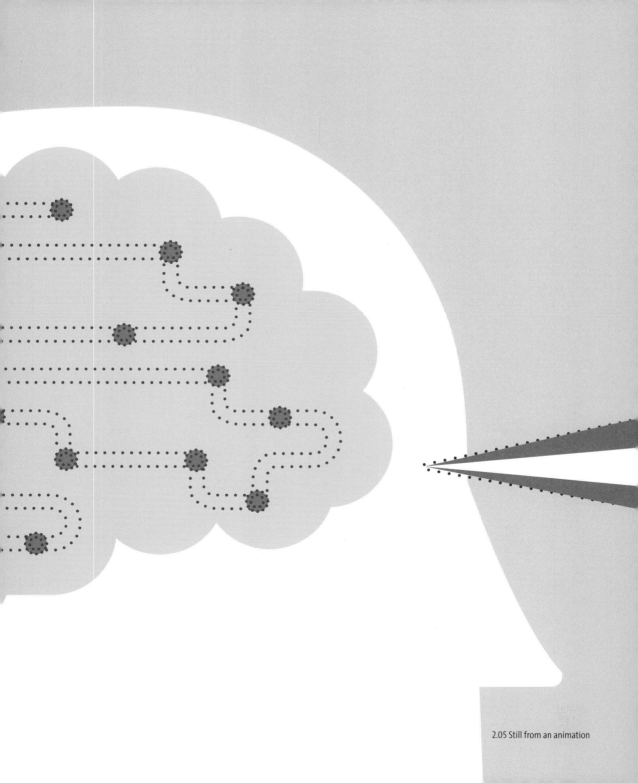

2.05 Still from an animation

The foundations of design are shaped by
↗ the psychology of perception and/or Gestalt psychology and Gestalt laws
↗ the neurosciences.

The Gestalt laws were formulated in the 19th century by German Gestalt psychologists based on empirical studies. The neuronal processes in perception did not come into the equation until the 20th century, above all through imaging techniques. Up to the present day, Gestalt laws are implemented in design praxis, but are also applied in the automated perception of objects using artificial intelligence.

Human perception comes from our five senses: seeing, hearing, smelling, touching and tasting. More than 50% of the human brain is used to analyze and interpret visual stimuli. Optical stimuli hit the retina of the eye, are translated into nerve impulses and processed by the brain. This sounds simple, but the exact way in which the brain processes optical information has not yet been fully researched. Not only the biological sensory system is involved in the process of perception, our previous experiences and our own psychological makeup play a role. In Constructivism, a philosophical school within epistemology, it was postulated that each of us "constructs" the world in our own head.

In one experiment, kittens were exposed for months to an environment consisting only of horizontal stripes. Afterwards, they were unable to perceive of vertical elements in a room such as chair legs and they bumped into them. As a result of the experiment conditions, their brains had not developed any direction-sensitive neurons that reacted to vertical stripes. So how we perceive something not only has to do with external stimuli, but also with our sensory system, which is shaped by our previous experiences.

Although it is clear that our brain reacts to perceptual stimuli and that its structure changes by being exposed to repetitive impressions, it is less known that we can also influence the neuronal plasticity of the brain, for example through meditation, which increases the density of neurons in the hippocampus. What that means is that we can change the way our brain works just by using the power of our imagination. If we allow our way of seeing things to be guided, we will see our surroundings with "new" eyes and to quote Wassily Kandinsky: "If the point of departure is correct and the direction well chosen, the goal cannot be missed".

Point

Although strictly speaking the point is not visible and has no form, its graphic quality is used as a circle to make certain statements about whether the point appears heavy or light within a square. If you add size and number as additional properties of points, the visual effect can be increased even further.

The ground forms a boundary frame and the stage for the figure. The above-mentioned figure-ground relationship is one of the most important principles of perception and provides the framework for other Gestalt laws, such as the laws of proximity, closure and continuity.

When there are a number of differently sized points, it is already possible to make statements, like competition and joy, for example, especially if the points are animated.

2.06 Graphic effect

1. harmonious

2. active / light

3. passive / heavy

4. forced calm

   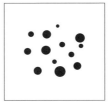

2.07 Competition / joy

The ability to abstract forms is fundamental for designers. We can already practice this with the help of the basic elements to be found on the human body. Joints and axes, such as the spine, the shoulder girdle and the position of the hips, are particularly helpful for representing the human body. The point here is to distinguish the essential from the unessential and to create meaning using only a few points.

So far, the "figure", in this case the point, has been placed without further syntactic restrictions on the "ground". In example 2.06 on the right, a 6x6 grid is given, which can make the positioning of the points lighter or heavier. It is not possible to achieve a state of harmony with only one point. In the 6x6 grid, it is not possible to position the point in the symmetrical center.

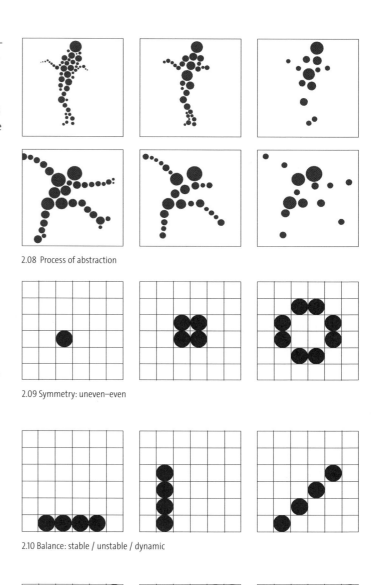

2.08 Process of abstraction

2.09 Symmetry: uneven–even

2.10 Balance: stable / unstable / dynamic

2.11 Contrast: much–little / light–dark / below–above

Analogy–the seasons

The following exercise introduces you to design with the help of analogies. Analogies always move within a certain frame of reference, which is based on similarities and shared properties.

The task here is to translate the four seasons with the help of points of different sizes. What do we normally think of when we imagine fall or winter? Falling leaves and bare trees? That would describe an analogy to nature. But this exercise is not about depicting falling leaves or a bare tree using points, it is about finding a system that is completely free of iconographic representation, using graphic analogies instead.

Throughout the world there are different definitions of seasons, which refer only to some extent to temperature differences. The indigenous people of the Yolngu, Aborigines in northern Australia, refer to six seasons, and in tropical countries the seasons are differentiated into the rainy and dry seasons.

Different graphic analogies can be found for each of the respective definitions.

What is important, is that the respective seasons also define themselves well via our physical, social and emotional reactions. For example, in the 4 Seasons model, we are happy about the first rays of spring sunshine after a cold winter, we might become more active and feel the new rising energy in us. In summer, nothing can hold us back, and many people enjoy being outside. When the rays of the sun start to get weaker, we already start to adapt towards winter again in the dull days of autumn and our energy levels often drop as a result.

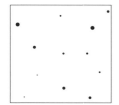   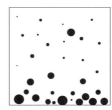

2.12 Analogy between temperature differences and human reactions: winter / spring / summer / fall

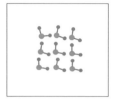
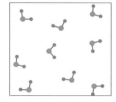

2.13 The physical states of water molecules:
solid / liquid / gaseous

Physics can also serve as an interculturally neutral analogy and explanatory model for visualization. Water (H₂O) is suitable for our example, as it is the most important molecule for all life and temperature differences can be easily represented by depicting its different physical states.

At low temperatures, less than 0°C/32°F, water molecules form a solid body (ice). They then sit on their grid positions, vibrating around their resting position. If heat is supplied to the solid, the vibration velocity increases, and this happens every time the temperature increases. By the time the melting temperature of 0°C/32°F is reached, the molecules have changed to the liquid state. If the water is further heated up to boiling point at 100°C/ 212°F, more and more molecules change over to the gaseous state.

When heat is supplied, the molecules rise upwards and when things cool down, they sink downwards.

Transfer to the point size:
↗ small points: cold, little movement
↗ large points: warm, a lot of movement

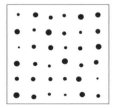
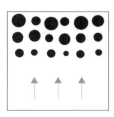
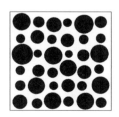
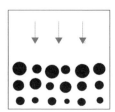

2.14 Analogy to physics
Winter: ice as a solid body
Spring: heat supply
Summer: gaseous state
Fall: cooling

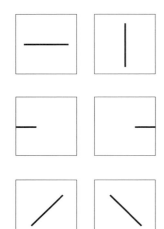

2.15 Effects of the line
stable / unstable
coming in / going out
rising / falling

Line

The line is of measurable length, but mathematically it has no width. It results from the movement of the point and is never static. Points focus the gaze, while lines direct it. The simplest line is a straight line, the horizontal line. It is stable and tension-free in contrast to the vertical, which appears unstable. This can be easily understood by looking at architecture: a flat building appears more stable than a skyscraper. After the right angle, the diagonal makes use of the 45-degree angle and is therefore the third simple straight line. Interestingly, certain neurons in the primary visual cortex are assigned to these three directions, i.e. some react preferentially to horizontal lines, others to vertical lines and again others to diagonal lines.

The line has a much greater variety in its syntactic means than the point. We can use it to represent almost anything: e.g. characters, floor plans and landscapes.

The great expressiveness of the line is also interculturally effective, which is shown

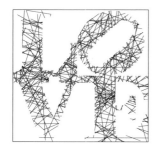 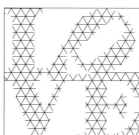  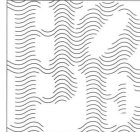

2.16 Interpretation of the artwork LOVE by American Pop Art artist Robert Indiana, 1966

by an experiment with the two contrary fantasy words "Takete" and "Maluma". The exercise is to assign these to a pointed or soft form.

It has to do with the sound of words and that there is a connection between sound and meaning. This is also referred to as 'sound symbolism'. As such, when developing logos consisting of letters, care is taken to ensure that they sound pleasant and that the writing matches them, as in the case of Coca-Cola, which was developed in 1886 and has hardly changed since.

The renowned Bauhaus teacher and painter Kandinsky used the dynamics of the body in the expressive dance of the 1920s, for example to depict "the energetic development of the diagonal".

2.17 Examples from my teaching using the Takete-Maluma duo

Top: 1st semester with German students

Below: Design students from different study courses in Solo, Indonesia

2.18 Wassily Kandinsky, "Dance Curves: On the Dances of Palucca", 1926

The line in movement

Asian and Arab calligraphy strives for a beauty of form that goes far beyond pure legibility. Transmitting information is of secondary importance, more important is the entire creative process, starting with mixing the ink as a meditative introduction to the calm, flowing movement of the hand and arm, which makes perfect line management possible in the first place. The brush represents the extension of the hand, so that the physical movement and the visual expression correspond, in a very similar way to dance.

In this animation exercise, you first decide what line style you want to use and then, so that you have a choice, you create a set of characters over a geometrically constructed matrix. In the course of this exercise, you will realize how critical selection is to the visual quality of the animation. It is almost impossible to animate complex, angled or cumbersome lines harmoniously and to bring them into concise shapes. The semi-circular line (2.21), however, offers a varied spectrum of individual forms.

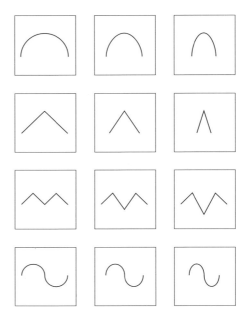

2.19 Matrix for creating a character set

2.20 Storyboard using the line as form: half ellipses

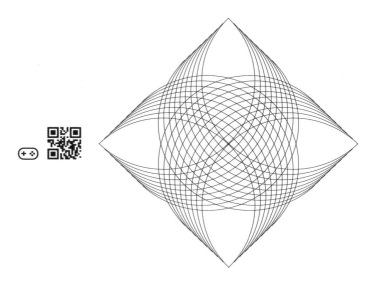

2.21 Individual pictures from an animation layered on top of one another

Important factors in animation:

↗ The influence of the form and the size of the line on the overall effect

↗ The flowing movement of all forms, without a line coming to a standstill — even if the velocity might be different

↗ The dissolution of concise forms should correspond to physical systems of reference like the centrifugal force, which can dissolve rotating forms through the rotational movement

↗ Velocity and braking to reinforce the effect of becoming stronger

Plane

The surface is the first basic element that is suited for a practical design test. It has a closed form across a surface area that is the carrier of information.

A series of lines that are stacked, as it were, one on top of the other, result in a rectangular plane, and yet of the three basic forms, the circle is always mentioned first. It occupies first place in the history of human development. Small children begin at the age of about 2 to scribble circular shapes and rotational swirls. Not until later do they include closed shapes with round contours and rectangular shapes in their repertoire.

The circle is one of the oldest symbols in human history. It does not have a beginning or an end, nor does it have direction or orientation, and it is often seen as a symbol for eternity, for infinity. The square is a static, stable, rational form and constructed with right angles. It stands for a principle of order created by humans. The last basic form, the triangle, stands for hierarchical systems and religious principles such as the Trinity: God the Father, the Son, and the Holy Spirit; or Shiva, Brahma and Vishnu. It also has a strong symbolic character in the three-dimensional pyramid. From an intercultural point of view, it is the most exciting and dynamic basic form.

Only the surface as a two-dimensional, closed form has the property of displaying different brightness and color, so that it stands out from the ground, is easily recognizable thanks to a clear contrast ratio and can act as a sign.

Logos are particularly suitable when it comes to assessing their visual conciseness. They are the most important identification feature for a company and should, of course, also be easy to identify from a distance and be easily recognizable in both small and large formats. If a logo is applied to a pane of glass, for example, its compact form must be able to withstand the background.

III BASIC FORMS

IV DESIGN QUALITY

CIRCLE
endless, dynamic,
in motion

RECTANGLE
stable, sets boundaries,
neutral and calm when a square

TRIANGLE
active, shows direction,
hierarchical

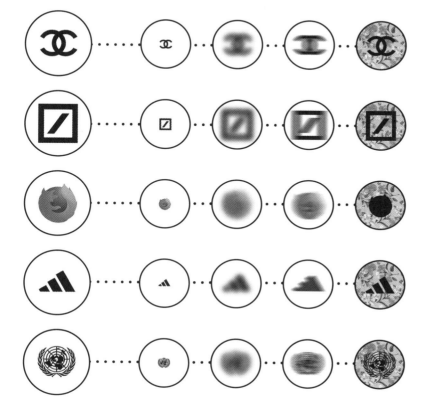

Logo quality test
Syntactic criteria for
the sign quality

↗ Scalability
↗ Impact from a distance
↗ Resistance to the
  background

2.22 Basic forms and quality criteria

"Good Design"

Is there such a thing as a "good design"? What exactly is meant by it and is this term – which was coined in the 1950s – not long since outdated? The Swiss artist, architect, designer and Bauhaus student Max Bill, as well as the renowned American graphic designer Raul Rand and others, devoted themselves almost simultaneously to the credo of simplicity, functionality and timelessness.

This period of Functionalism was followed by countercurrents that can be attributed to Postmodernism. Emotion and fantasy became socially acceptable again and let the design world breathe a sigh of relief, as if liberated from an overly tight corset made of design premises.

Logos that once seemed to be carved in stone have become flexible today and are adapted to fit in with different applications and messages. The working world of designers is also marked by flexibility; they work in workspaces that are not tied to one location and form global networks together.

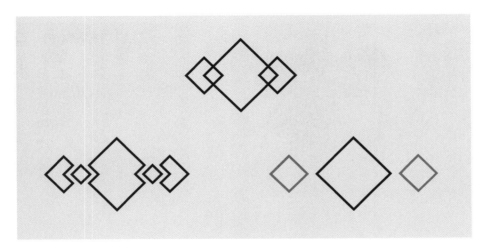

2.23 Law of continuity

Design solutions are the outcome of different social and economic conditions and no longer have universal validity in the international context. The way in which we perceive things is, of course, subject to change, but the Gestalt laws and the basic principles governing perception are intercultural. This connects us beyond the constantly changing aspects of style.

2.24 HAL Tube Stackable, Vitra, Jasper Morrison, 2010

2.25 Malaysian bicycle rickshaws, known as "Bejaks"

2.26 Hans (Nick) Roericht, Stacking tableware TC 100, Design 1958/59

Point, line and plane in everyday life
In addition to geometric shapes such as pentagons, hexagons, octagons, etc., there are of course amorphous shapes as well, which we have not included here. When training our sense of perception, it is much more important to apply our new visual experiences to everyday life and to become more sensitive to what is all around us. Where do we see round forms, where do we see square forms and what do they tell us? This might be done during a walk in the countryside or in the city; in the latter case, architecture and outdoor advertising play a role.

2.27 Apple logo,
1977, by Rob Janoff

The Apple logo has been at the top of the Interbrand rankings to date. It is still stylish, even though it was developed in the 1970s and hasn't changed in its basic form since then. What effect does it have on us? Is it perhaps a little cheeky? When Steve Jobs saw it for the first time, he is said to have just smiled and nodded, but didn't say much. The logo depicts a bitten apple, but that's not all. It is also very geometric, round and harmonious, making it timeless.

2.28 Logo of the
Deutsche Bank, 1974,
by Anton Stankowski

If we look at the logo of the Deutsche Bank, for example, it shouldn't be that difficult for us to describe its visual impact either. What do the square and the diagonal convey? It's not important for us to know what the bank wanted to express with the logo, nor is it about defining the exact effect it has on us. What is important here is that we find a way into the basic elements and forms used in logos. We now know that the square stands for stability and the diagonal for dynamics.

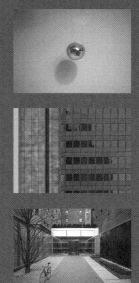
2.29 Point, line and plane

Daniela Kirchlechner, Berlin

Studied Visual Communication at the University of the
Arts Berlin and the University of Applied Arts Vienna
Established "mitte" and "up-designers berlin-wien"
Since 2008 lecturer at the University of Applied Sciences
Anhalt, Campus Bauhaus Dessau. Since 2020 professor
at Münster School of Design

Alternative teaching
Holistic thinking, researching, analytical working
and documenting in the "Basic Gestaltungs-Labor"
(Basic Design Laboratory).

Learning goals
↗ Developing a design vocabulary in praxis
↗ Working out a theoretical basis
↗ Sensitization of perception and perceptual phenomena

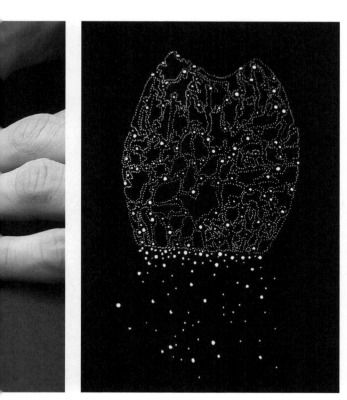

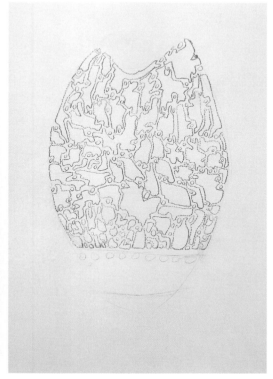

2.30 Points in a serial layout | Scattering, compression, accentuation

Daniela Kirchlechner, Berlin

From two-dimensional to three-dimensional

Assignment
"Draw" a three-dimensional object using wire and
present it in a setting using light and shade!

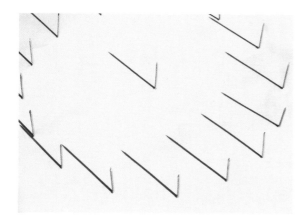
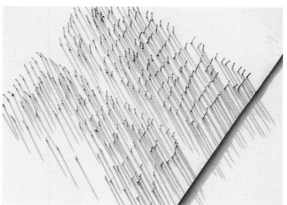

2.31 The line in space – light and shade | Giving form, light + shade + photographic composition

միջազգային

Armenian

دولي

Arabic

בינלאומי

Hebrew (Israel)

インターナショナル

Katakana (Japan)

ዓለም አቀፍ

Amharic (Ethiopia, Eritrea)

international

Latin

საერთაშორისო

Georgian

国際

Hanzi (China)

международный

Cyrillic (Russia, Eastern Europe)

διεθνές

Greek

국제

Hangul (Korea)

अंतरराष्ट्रीय

Devanagari (Brahmic scripts)

TYPE AND FORM

Type encompasses the totality of the characters within a graphic information system. The information itself is encoded using the system and readers must possess the code to understand the information conveyed. But who invented the first of these graphic sytems, and when did that occur?

The first tangible means of communicating information with two- and three-dimensional characters includes some of the oldest cultural artifacts of humanity. The history of their emergence is as long and controversial as the lineage of humanity itself. The oldest pictorial symbols, simple engravings in mussel shells, are half a million years old.[1] Cave paintings with handprints and realistic hunting scenes depicting animals, people and even hybrid creatures have been dated to over 40,000 years old. What they mean is unclear. One hypothesis is that they had a ritual meaning and told stories.[2]

Writing systems became necessary as the societal structures of human communities became ever more complex. In the Neolithic Revolution, nomadic hunter-gatherer communities gradually transitioned to practicing farming and animal husbandry in agrarian settlements over a long period stretching from about 10000 to 5000 BCE. The domestication of animals and technical innovations, such

alphabetical

syllabic

morphosyllabic

3.01 The word "international" in common international scripts.

as the plough and improved systems for food storage, created opportunities to pursue other activities. This engendered the ability to produce more food than consumed, increased population, and new, emerging occupations, such as potter and blacksmith.[3] From about 5000 BCE onwards, rigorously organized city states began to form from small villages. Barter systems flourished and writing systems developed to simplify trade and optimize administrative processes. Forerunners of the writing systems used today emerged independently in different locations around the world. The great cultures of antiquity, in Mesopotamia, Egypt and China, as well as the Maya and the cultures of the Indus valley, all used sophisticated type systems.

The first writing system, cuneiform, was probably invented by the Sumerians in Mesopotamia, in what is now Iraq, over 5,000 years ago. This system was very popular and was in continuous use across all of the Middle East from the 2nd century BCE. It initially consisted of pictograms i.e., stylized pictorial depictions of objects and living beings. Using pictograms is cumbersome and insufficient for complex communication. In time, people began to combine pictograms in such a way that they could also convey feelings, ideas and activities, thus forming what are known as ideograms. For example, the combination of pictograms for head and water meant drink, and the meaning of the symbol for foot was extended to mean both walking and standing, depending on the context.[4]

The rebus principle later came into play, and the same symbol could be both used for words that sounded similar, as well as for syllables and vowels. What was initially a pictographic type gradually developed into a partially phonetic type, where roughly 600 of the original 1,000 characters were sufficient.[5] Both the number of characters and their form were simplified. Round lines for iconographic symbols, such as the foot, gradually gave rise to straight lines and wedges, inscribed into soft clay with a stylus, pressed into the clay. Through time, the writing implement and the writing surface both continued to decisively influence developing forms of typography, as one can observe with the Roman stone inscriptions made with a chisel, or Arabic calligraphies drawn with a quill.

3100 BCE	3000 BCE	2400 BCE	1000 BCE

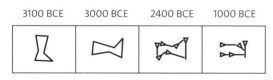

3.02 Cuneiform development, here the symbol, for "foot"

Over time, the growth of trade around the Mediterranean gave rise to the need for type that was easier to work with, giving rise to a phonetic type by the Phoenicians. The characters of this purely consonantal type were sequenced: in the first place was Aleph, the ox; the second, Beth, the house; and in third place Gimel, the camel's hump (alternatively, the throwing stick). There were 22 letters in all, written from left to right. The Phoenician predecessor to the Latin alphabet was born.

As the Phoenicians were merchants and seafarers, their innovation spread quickly across their trading territories and inspired the development of other alphabet types. The Aramaic, Hebrew, Arabic and Greek writing systems all derive from Phoenician type. The Greeks expanded the alphabet to 24 letters with the addition of vowels and thereby laid the foundation for the Latin and Cyrillic alphabets which followed, as well as the Germanic runes.

The Brahmi character set, predecessor of the Indian writing system, emerged some 2,500 years ago, presumably from the Aramaic, which in turn originated from the Phoenician alphabet. Brahmi was a combination of alphabetic and syllabic typography.

The first Chinese characters were pictograms. In contrast to other writing systems, the Chinese Hanzi and Japanese characters never employed a full abstraction of the characters into phonetic symbols (letters). Both these systems continue to be complex character systems encompassing pictograms, ideograms and phonograms.[6]

Today, Latin type is the most widespread writing system. Latin type is the primary type for 2.5 to 3.5 billion people, followed by Chinese type and characters from the Indian type family, with 1.5 billion users for each. Arabic and Cyrillic characters are the primary type for half a billion people each. And there are still languages, today, that are not written at all. Of some 7,000 [existing] languages, just under 4,000 of them have a written form.[7] The contemporary, unwritten languages are generally only spoken by a few hundred or thousand people each, and like many of the little-used written languages, face the threat of extinction.[8]

65

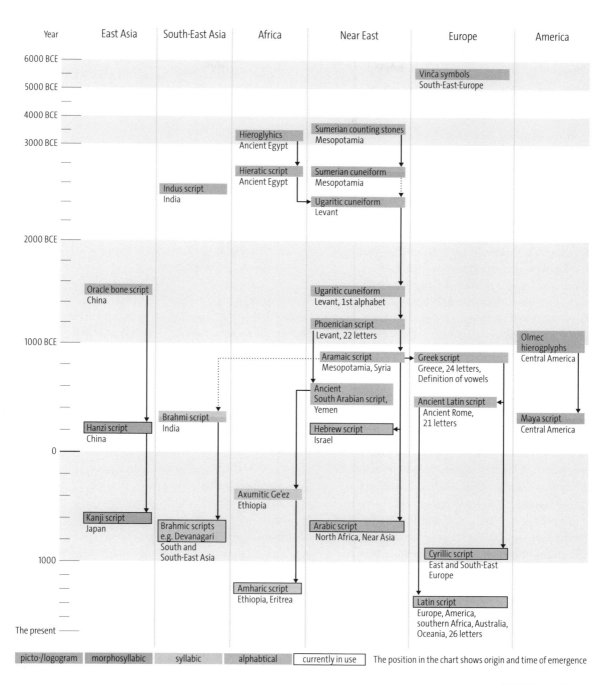

3.03 The history of script

Reading and type anatomy

Western culture as we know it today only came about in connection with the Greek and Latin alphabets. For centuries, right up until the 20th century, knowledge was mainly exchanged in written form. This changed over the course of the last century, as media and videos have come to play an ever-increasing role. Media theorist Marshall McLuhan already talked about the electronic age or the age images in the 1960s, and his vision of a "global village" – a technology-based community – predicted the Internet.[9] According to McLuhan, this would replace the printing age and therefore the predominance of type. The fact that people read and write more than ever before, especially on social media, was something he did not foresee. The style and length of texts have of course changed drastically depending on the medium, for example chat vs. email, something that is expressed clearly in McLuhan's famous words "The medium is the message".

How a piece of information is perceived and processed is different in different media. And how precisely the information is understood also changes. Types, unlike pictures, are developed in linear form – reading beginners read from letter to letter, while practiced readers read in so-called "saccades", that is, jumps that take in entire words or even groups of words. What is more, readers take in text chunks when reading, and if the text is not understood immediately, then the reader takes backward jumps.

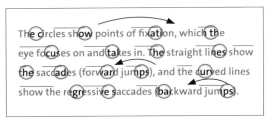

3.04 Reading process

Pictures, by comparison, are perceived of much faster and for longer, but also very differently from individual to individual.[10] However, legal texts, documenting history and poetry are only possible because letters can be produced with precision and the characters interpreted in a clear manner.

Typographic design requires some previous knowledge of the anatomy, type classification, type styles and the hierarchy of text elements such as copy text as well as main headings and subheading. The most important development in Latin type was the invention of movable lead type by Johannes Gutenberg (middle of the 15th century), although this was already known in Korea in the 13th century.[11]

Many of the technical terms used in typography are based on the lead letter and on letterpress printing. However, there was no uniform measuring system for type. It was not until three hundred years later in France that a uniform typographic system was established – the typographic point. This measures the point size of the lead letter, and this still applies today, even if analog letterpress printing is only used nowadays for very special graphic or artistic purposes. The American system, with its so-called pica point (1 pica point = 0.351 mm) has asserted itself as the norm due to desktop publishing and the corresponding software.

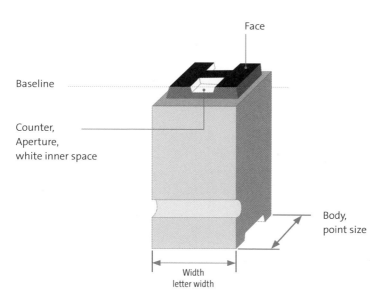

Face

Baseline

Counter,
Aperture,
white inner space

Body,
point size

Width
letter width

3.05 Important parts of the lead letter

Antiqua typefaces: 15th-19th century

Sans serif typefaces: from the 19th century

Aolgn

1	Serif	7	Cap height
2	Hairline	8	Ascender
3	Stem, Main stroke	9	x-height
4	Counter, Aperture	10	Descender
5	Axis	11	Body, point size
6	Bracketing	12	Baseline

3.06 Technical terms used in typography

Type classification

There are thousands of Latin typefaces[12] and it isn't easy to find your way around these to choose one. First, one can roughly divide faces into serif and sans serif fonts, that is, those with serifs and those without serifs. Beyond that, there are different classifications within the serif group such as Anglo-Saxon, French or German. Five main historical groups are presented here.[13]

Classification of Latin type began in 15th century Renaissance Europe. Fonts were often named for the highly respected letterpress printers and punch cutters who designed them. For example, Garamond, designed by Claude Garamond in the 16th century, is still very much in use today with many new editions. It is a French Renaissance antiqua, which spread across Europe quickly, due to its legibility, diverse variations and strength.

Didone established itself In the 18th century, following the French Revolution. It exhibits strong contrasts between its thick and thin strokes and comes across as cool, thanks to its angular serifs. The first printed cursive types, based on the strokes of a brush or quill, emerged at around the same time as one another.

Sans serif is a relatively new type classification, which first emerged at the beginning of the 19th century. Slab serif Egyptian came onto the market at around roughly the same time, during the Industrial Revolution. New products were advertised in newspapers and magazines using these heavy and striking serif faces.[14] The main developments of type classification were completed with these two type groups. Further developments were more of a technical nature, such as the spread of the open type format or the socalled variable fonts.

Sans Serif / Grotesque
1 Helvetica Regular
2 Frutiger Bold
3 The SansCd Bold

Serif / Humanist / Old Style
1 Garamond Italic
2 Bembo Regular
3 Centaur Swash

Serif / Modern
1 Bodoni Bold
2 Walbaum Bold Italic
3 Didot Bold

Slab Serif / Egyptienne
1 Rockwell Regular
2 Clarendon Light
3 American Typewriter Regular

3.07 Font examples

Script
1 Edwardian Script
2 Monoline Script
3 Kuenstler Script

A B C

D E F

G H I

J K L

M n O

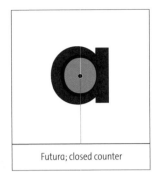

Futura; closed counter

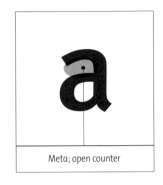

Meta; open counter

Futura; single-story

Meta; double-story

3.08 Comparing counters and loops in type

Legibility

The legibility of Latin as well as other typefaces depends on proportions and spacing. If the counters (the interior open space of the letter) are too small, or the x-heights too diminutive, in relation to the cap heights, then reading becomes difficult, especially in small-print texts like those used in forms. But if the letters are too similar, this risks making the letters difficult to distinguish from one another, as can be seen in the single-story hook of the minuscules (lowercase letters) of Futura.

Basically, many rules in design have to do with maintaining adequate spacing. There are good reasons to make manual adjustments to letter spacing in headlines and titles, and it's obligatory in logos. An example is the typographic logo for NIVEA. It aims to be striking and memorable. The visually identical spaces improve readability and create an even overall look.

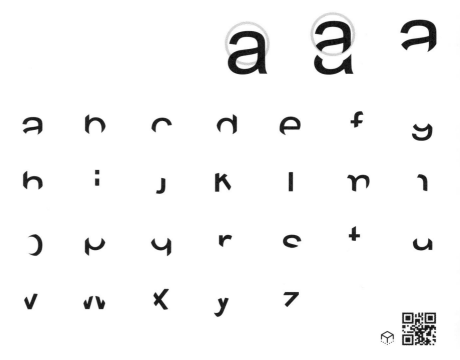

3.09 Exercise: restrictions to legibility

Letter shapes are subject to the same laws of perception as other forms. Distort type as little as you would copyright-protected photos. Every font has its own character, but the primary goal of its design is to achieve its communications objective. In his ten commandments of type, one of the most important German designers of the 20th century, Kurt Weidemann, said the following: "Bad type [in general] is antisocial."[15] Clear words that are very much in contrast to Paula Scher's approach: "It's through mistakes that you can actually grow. You have to get bad in order to get good." She was the first female partner in Pentagram[16], New York. In no other area of design do rules and very divergent criteria for making aesthetic judgments play such a significant role as in typography.

It makes sense to first examine the formal aspects of a typeface and to research which elements are necessary for good legibility. A careful balancing of and sensitivity to detail are among the key skills of typography.

3.10 The tonal weight of type in differing values of gray

Hierarchical systems of tonal weight and negative space

Every sample of text has its own specific quality of gray, which you can easily see
by squinting your eyes until your vision blurs. Achieve a similar effect using Photoshop's Blur Effect. Seeing in this way helps us perceive what is essential and what is
not through the *color* of the typography. Important texts are bold, and a headline
is often bigger than the rest of the copy. In more elaborate designs, like those for
magazines and websites, it makes sense to use a hierarchical system that specifies
all text functions. If you want to structure a text, then this will include issues of
spacing, as between paragraphs, degrees of indentation, for bulleted lists, etc.
With the entire page in mind, you design the negative spaces.

However, if something needs a gentle emphasis, like a special term or an author's
name, like Johannes Gutenberg, then small capitals, or italics with a similar tonal
weight to the copytext may be used – for example, *Johannes Gutenberg*.

Look and feel

Typefaces are a powerful tool, as they always transport two messages: an informative one and an emotional one. Decorative lettering is not suitable for a factual report, and Arial is not the right type for a wedding invitation. Type speaks a visual language, and each face has its own character and conveys a distinct impression. We must make use of this when addressing different target groups.

Since the 1970s, many companies have commissioned font designers to create a corporate font specifically for their company; examples include Audi, BBC, Coca Cola and YouTube Sans.[17] The emotional impact of a typeface is often underestimated. It's probably the most-used and most-often perceived brand component – even if this sometimes happens subliminally. Every piece of text information in the incisive, proprietary font of a company is an emotional point of contact between the brand and its target audience (referred to as the brand touchpoint). Type design most likely provides the highest return among corporate design investments, as it is only created once.

3.11 Typography and target group

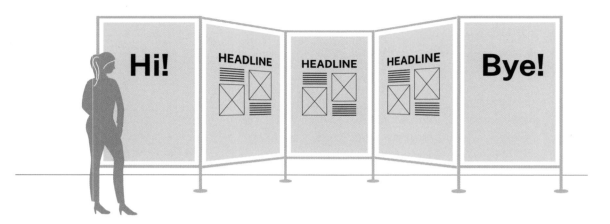

3.12 Dos and don'ts in larger dimension designs

Type in space

Consider the third dimension in designing
for packaging and large installations, like trade
shows, conferences and exhibits. The most
important thing to note here is the real scale
of the object bearing the information, such
as exhibition display panels. Dimensionality must
be experienced. Texts should be tested by printing
them at actual size. If this is not done, then there
is a risk that the information, whether text or
image, may not be easily read or deciphered.

Important Dos and Don'ts:

↗ Dimensions and proportions must
   be true to scale
↗ Lighting/ambience (in the space)
↗ Materials and material combinations
↗ The surrounding spatial background
   (this may compete with the design, and
   influence it positively or negatively)
↗ Focus on graphic elements & colors in
   the context of the space and lighting
↗ Reading height

↗ Design – the more compelling, the better!
↗ Short content is better than long:
   Use compact texts
↗ Guide the eye using typographic hierarchies,
   pictures and graphic elements (lines, etc.)
↗ Basic grid: alignment should
   underlie all elements

↗ The type is too small!

↗ The type and images are positioned too low down for an adult to see or too high up for a child. If this is the case, your design will not properly address any of the target groups!

↗ Type and image are far too high up!

3.13 Architectural model of
German Embassy in
Tiflis, by Wulf Architekten,
Stuttgart, Germany

Saki Mafundikwa, Zimbabwe

Saki Mafundikwa is a visionary who gave up a successful design career in New York to return to his home country of Zimbabwe, opening its first graphic design and new media school. He owes his international renown to the publication of "African Alphabets", which provides a comprehensive overview of Afrikan writing systems. He has participated in exhibitions and workshops all over the world, given lectures, and contributed to a wide range of publications on the globalization of design and African aesthetics.

The logo of the Black Documentary Collective is inspired by the murals of the Ndebele women of Zimbabwe. In it, bold black lines frame circles and semicircles.

In his contribution to the "Tolerance Traveling Poster Show", Mafundikwa uses lit candles to design the word "Kunzwisisana", which means "understand" in Shona, the Zimbabwean Bantu language.

The Bantu pictograph script is used only by healers, elders and women. Each character expresses a word or idea. This script is one of over 20 that Mafundikwa recorded for posterity in his signal work.

3.15 Tolerance Traveling Poster Show, 2017

BLACK DOCUMENTARY COLLECTIVE

3.14 Logo design, 2017

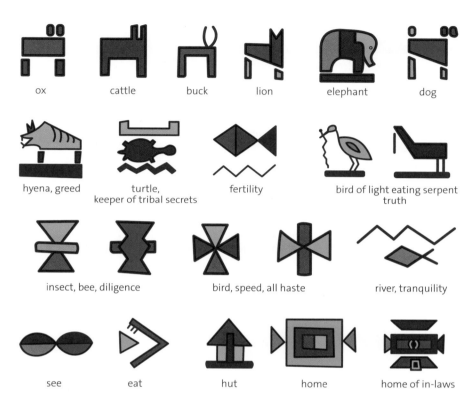

ox	cattle	buck	lion	elephant	dog

hyena, greed	turtle, keeper of tribal secrets	fertility	bird of light eating serpent truth

insect, bee, diligence	bird, speed, all haste	river, tranquility

see	eat	hut	home	home of in-laws

3.16 Afrikan Alphabets: Bantu Symbol Writing, and below, Script, 2006

Anushka Sani, India

Anushka Sani founded her "Thought Over Design" studio, in Mumbai, in 2014. She studied Visual Communication Design and Mass Media at the Srishti School of Art, Design & Technology in Bengaluru, India, before later becoming Creative Director of Skarma. She conducted design workshops at the INK conference, Goa & ISDI, Mumbai and is a guest juror at the Ecole School of Design, in Mumbai. Her vision integrates global standards into design processes and improves the quality and value of design in India.

One focus of the agency is on branding and packaging design. Their approach to design is strongly conceptual, particularly evident in their logo development, where design style is based on the target group, integrating hand-drawn shapes with fonts, as in the logo of "samaaru".

3.17 Branding and logo design, 2019

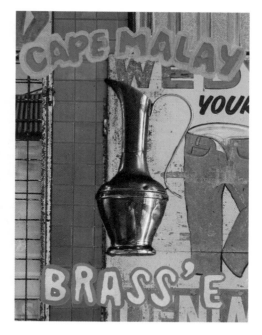

3.18 Experimental design, 2020

Thaakierah Abdul, South Africa

Thaakierah Abdul is among the Cape Malays of South Africa, decended from Southeast Asian slaves. As a black Muslim woman, she simultaneously expresses her identity and protest through the design of collages and posters. She deals with topics including ethnic and class affiliation, exclusion and politics. Abdul brings these topics to the page with strong, high contrast colors and hand-made typography, drawing attention to the exclusion of many population groups in South Africa, often through gentrification.

The South African custom of using recycled materials in an artful and colorful way, like wallpapering with newspapers and painting store signs by hand, is palpable in both these posters. The outline fonts, in saturated primary and secondary colors, integrate organically into each composition.

Seduction

SEDUCTION:
FORM,
SENSATION,
AND
THE
PRODUCTION
OF
ARCHITECTURAL
DESIRE
A SYMPOSIUM
JANUARY 19–20, 2007

A decade of explosive development in communication and information retrieval technologies, from Bluetooth to GPS and Blackberries to iPods, has produced a global datascape where the ability to access information, anywhere, and at anytime, is nearly ubiquitous. The alliance of this data-saturated scenario with similar advances in computational, material, and fabrication technologies requires the field of architecture to question its historic presumption as an embodiment of meaningful content—regardless of its specific posturing as icon, sign, or index.

Through presentations given by a select group of architects, critics, theorists, and innovators this symposium will explore how architecture is shedding its burden of communication in favor of new formal ambitions, including the customization of moods, the influences of sensation, and the emergence of a new species of irrefutably contemporary aesthetics.

**FRIDAY
JANUARY 19, 2007
3:30 PM**

WELCOME
Robert A.M. Stern

MAKING APPEARANCES

Introduction
Ben Pell
Architect,
Yale University

Herbert Muschamp
Critic
Peggy Phelan
Performance Theorist,
Stanford University
Gregory Crewdson
Photographer,
Yale University
Jeffrey Kipnis
Theorist,
Ohio State University

Response
Sarah Whiting
Theorist,
Princeton University

**FRIDAY
JANUARY 19, 2007
6:30 PM**

KEYNOTE
Sylvia Lavin
Theorist,
University of California,
Los Angeles
"As If"

RECEPTION
Architecture Gallery
2nd floor
A&A Building

**SATURDAY
JANUARY 20, 2007
9:30 AM**

WELCOME
Mark Foster Gage
Architect, Yale University

PRACTICING SEDUCTION

Introduction
Henry Urbach
Curator,
San Francisco MoMA

Herman Diaz-Alonso
Architect,
Southern California
Institute of Architecture,
Columbia University
David Erdman
Architect,
University of California,
Los Angeles
Mark Foster Gage
Architect,
Yale University
Kivi Sotamaa
Architect,
Ohio State
University

Response
Peter Eisenman
Architect,
Yale University

**SATURDAY
JANUARY 20, 2007
1:15 PM**

FORMS OF SEDUCTION

Introduction
Edward Mitchell
Architect,
Yale University

Roemer Van Toorn
Theorist,
Berlage Institute
Sanford Kwinter
Theorist,
Rice University
Greg Lynn
Architect,
Yale University
Chrissie Iles
Curator,
Whitney Museum
of American Art

Response
Mark Linder
Theorist,
Syracuse University

Concluding
Conversation
Gregory Crewdson
Peter Eisenman
Chrissie Iles
Sylvia Lavin

RECEPTION
Architecture Gallery
2nd floor
A&A Building

YALE SCHOOL
OF ARCHITECTURE
A & A Building
Hastings Hall
(basement floor)
180 York Street,
New Haven, CT

This
symposium
is free,
but
reservations
are required
prior to
January 12,
2007.
Phone
203.432.2889
or email
archevents@
yale.edu.

The Yale
School of
Architecture
is a Registered
Provider with
The American
Institute of
Architects
Continuing
Education
Systems.
Credit earned
by attending
this symposium
will be reported
to CES Records
for AIA members.
Certificates
of Completion
for non-AIA
members
are available
upon request.

3.19 Seduction, cooperation with Michael Bierut, 2006

Marian Bantjes, Canada

Marian Bantjes is a designer, typographer, author and illustrator. She lives in Canada and works as a typesetter and was one of the co-founders of the Digitopolis studio. She has worked as an independent artist and typographer since 2003. Her work has been published in over 100 books and magazines worldwide. She has served as a juror for many different prizes such as the D&AD (UK) and ADC (NY). She became a member of the Alliance Graphique Internationale (AGI) in 2008 and her book "I Wonder" appeared in 2010. "Pretty Pictures" — a comprehensive monograph of her work was published in 2013.

Banjtje's works show ornate decorations, wrought arabesques, intertwined patterns and ornaments. All are designed manually and Bantjes sometimes integrates natural materials into her pieces. She has a preference for baroque forms and curved lines, which she arranges in numerous variations, each different and fresh.

Banjtje writes, "…I don't believe that less is more,"[18] contradicting the words of famed 2oth century architect, Mies van der Rohe. He postulated that less is more and, with his Bauhaus colleagues, coined an axiom that endures to this day. Bantjes has created a unique, complex style that boldly stands up to this maxim, in both words and design (see the Speak Up blog).

3.20 The Girl Show, 2005

3.21 Saks heart, 2008

Elizabeth Resnick, USA

Elizabeth Resnick is an emeritus professor at the Massachusetts College of Art and Design, in Boston, USA, and has run the Graphic Design course there. She gained her B.F.A. and M.F.A. in Graphic Design at the Rhode Island School of Design, USA. From 1989-2005, she was a board member of the Professional Association for Design (AIGA) in Boston and was recipient of the AIGA Boston's Fellows' Award in 2007. She is a passionate design curator and has organized extensive design exhibitions. Her publications include exhibition catalogs and graphic design textbooks, as well as articles in renowned graphic design magazines. She is actively engaged in the areas of Social Design and human rights.

The four elements: black background, white circle, red, tilted square, and a line of type struggle for a harmonious balance. The red square is positioned within the white circle in such a way that it could turn at any time—its diagonal axis makes it appear unbalanced.

The text line is set horizontally, and thus normally, but it too seems to be in motion. The colors utilized, red, white and black, are the most common colors in all languages of the world and convey a high degree of concision.

The overall composition presents a high level of tension. The theme of immigration is staged as a balancing act, via creative use of minimal means.

3.22 Immigration poster, 2014

Gustavo Greco, Brazil

Gustavo Greco, born in 1974, is the founder and Creative Director of Greco Design in Belo Horizonte. He studied at the Pontifícia Universidade Católica de Minas Gerais, Brazil and now teaches in the post-Baccalaureate program in Brand Management at the IEC - Instituto de Educação Continuada. He often acts as a judge at large international design festivals, representing Brazil in the juries. Since 2000, Greco has been chosen for every issue of the Bienal Nacional de Design Gráfico (ADG Brazil) and has received many accolades, including the Grand Prix of the Red Dot Design Award and the London International Awards.

The typeface on the left poster is a decorative, hanwritten font, and thus expresses something personal. It's red hue expresses a call-to-action. The second poster uses a bold, contructed sans-serif. High attention is achieved by its crossed out letters. Because of the strikethrough, the meaning of the statement changes from. "Whoever loves, does not kill" to "Whoever loves, loves".

3.24 Poster "Quem Ama não Mata?", 2019

3.23 Poster "Design Meets Fa.vela", 2019

Susana Machicao, Bolivia

Susana Machicao was born in Bolivia in 1968. She studied at the Universidad Católica Boliviana "San Pablo" and founded "Machicao design" in 1999. She is founder and director of Bolivian Graphic Designers, the Latin American Design Project and the project "Women Designers". She occupies a leading position at the Bolivian poster Biennial BICeBé, the Biennial for Latin American typography Tipos Latinos, and sits on the council of ambassadors of Latin American design at the University of Palermo in Argentina, among others.

The llama is a typical farm animal in Bolivia and appears in multiple motifs within this poster series. The llama is portrayed made of leaves with a diamond patterns, a silhouette, and a lacey, floral motif. The accompanying typography displays an equally rich degree of variation, with a renaissance antiqua, two different cursive fonts and a constructed sans-serif.

3.25 Poster for Conferences, 2016: La Collanga en SantaCruz, La Boliviana en Cali / La Boliviana en San Luis Potosi / La Boliviana en Asuncion

Georgios D. Matthiopoulos

Studied Graphic Design at the C.S.U. Los Angeles and Printing
Technology at the London College of Printing
Founding member of the Greek Font Society
Since 1990 lecturer at the University of West Attica
Translations: Robert Bringhurst's,
Elements of Typographical Style (2001)
Author: Anthology of Greek Typography (2009)

Greek letters

The Phoenicians invented the first alphabetic writing system with only a handful of consonants. This was adopted by the Greeks, who added symbols for vowels, thus developing a formidable writing tool that helped them reach hitherto unrivaled achievements. In Antiquity, the Greeks used majuscule letters, while the writing direction was only formalized from left to right in the 5th BCE.

The 7th BCE Greek colonization of Southern Italy introduced their alphabet there, leading to the development of the Latin script in Western Europe. Because they are both variants of a common predecessor, the Latin alphabet closely resembles the Greek one in the majuscule, and they share the letters A, B, E, H, I, K, M, N, O, P, T, Y, X, Z, although some do not have the same vocal value. The other Greek characters are Γ, Δ, Θ, Λ, Ξ, Π, Σ, Φ, Ψ, Ω. The shape of the letters was monoline throughout Antiquity, while stroke modulation and serifs appeared later, influenced by the Roman paradigm.

During the Byzantine era, scribes gradually reshaped the letters into miniscule forms with hundreds of alternatives, ligatures and abbreviations. And in the early 9th century, Cyrillic script was also developed based on the Greek alphabet and applied for the Slavic languages.

Phoenician alphabet	Early Greek alphabet	5th c. Greek alphabet	5th c. Roman alphabet

3.26 Schematic evolution of the early Greek and Latin alphabets from the Phoenician progenitor

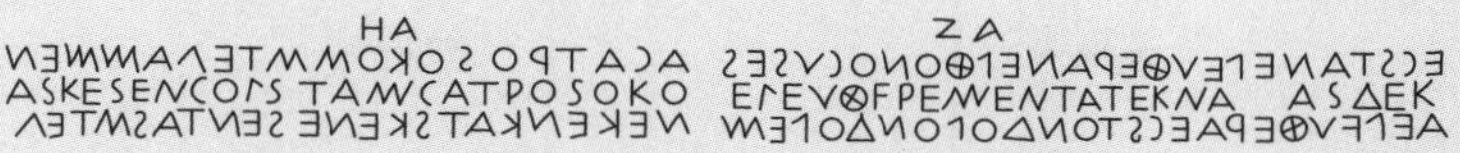

ΗΑ
ΝΕΜΜΑΛΕΤΜΟΚΣΟΟΥΒΑΟ ΑΣΑΤΡΟΣΟΚΑΤΡΟΣΟΚΟ ΖΑ ΕΣΣΤΑΝΕΥΘΕΡΑΝΕΘΟΦΘΟΝΟΥΣΕΣ ΕΝΟΟΟΘΕΝΑΤΕ
ΑΣΚΕΣΕΝΟΟΓΣ ΤΑΜΣΑΤΡΟΣΟΚΟ ΕΓΕΝΘΦΓΡΕΜΕΝΤΑΤΕΚΝΑ ΑΣΔΕΚ
ΜΕΚΕΝΚΑΤΣΚΕΝΕΣΕΝΤΑΣΜΤΕΝ ΑΕΓΥΘΕΡΒΑΕΣΣΤΟΝΔΙΟΛΑΝΟΟΥΝ

5th BCE Gortyna codes, Crete

ΕΝΕΣΕΣΑΘΕΝΑΙΟΙΚΡΑΤΟΣ
ΜΕΛΕΣΘΑΙΔΕΑΥΙΟΑΘΕΝΕΣ
ΤΟΣΠΡΥΤΑΝΕΣΚΑΙΤΕΜΒΟΛΕ
ΝΟΝΔΕΤΕΣΙΑΛΛΕΣΙΠΟΛΕΣΙΝΟ

5th BCE, Greek stele

ΑΒΓΔΕΖΗΘΙΚΛΜΝΞΟΠΡΣΤΥΦΧΨΩ

4th BCE, Greek letters

ΑΒΓΔΕΖΗΘΙΚΛΜΝΞΟΠΡΣΤΥΦΧΨΩ

1st c., Greek letters

αβγδεζηθικλμνξοπρστυφχψω

2nd c., Papyrus 46

ΑΒΓΔΕΖΗΘΙΚΛΜΝΞΟΠΡΥΤΥΦΧΨΩ

5th c., Codex Alexandrinus

ΑΒΓΔΕΖΗΘΙΚΛΜΝΞΟΠΡΣΤΥΦΧΨΩ

ΑΒΓΔΕΖΗΘΙΚΛΜΝΞΟΠΡΣΤΥΦΧΨΩ

6-8th c., Greek letters

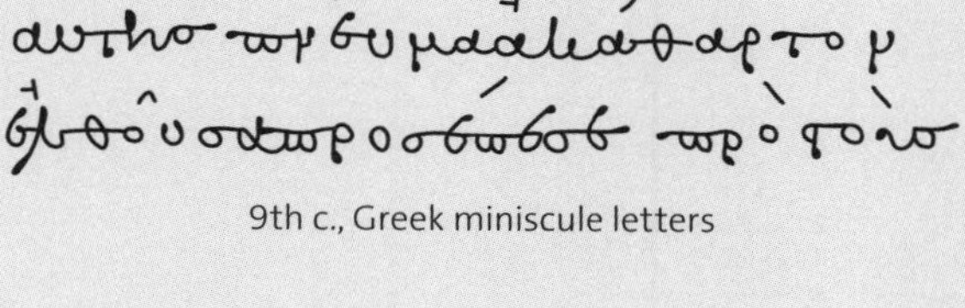

αυτου hoξχετοθυγατριου
αυτω πρ ευμααλιαθαρτορ
θεου οσταοροσθωθοθ προ τοιω

9th c., Greek miniscule letters

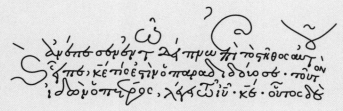

14th c., Greek miniscule letters

ΑΒΓΔΕΖΗΘΙΚΛΜΝΞΟΠΡΣΤΥΦΧΥΩ

1494, Greek – Aldus Manutius / Francesco Griffo (Venice)

ΑΒΓΔΕΖΗΘΙΚΛΜΝΞΟΠΡΣΤΥΦΧΨΩ

1499, Greek – Nicolaos Vlastos / Zacharias Kalliergis (Venice)

ΑΒΓΒΔΒΕΒΖΒΗΘΙΚΛΜΝΞΟΠΡΣΤΥΦΧΨΩΩ

1544, Grecs du roi – Angelos Vergikios / Claude Garamond (Paris)

Gutenberg's invention of printing in the 1450s occurred when the weakened Byzantine Empire fell to the advancing Ottoman Turks. It was the same period in which the Renaissance was emerging in Italy. Many Greek scholars went to Italy to teach, contributing towards the development of Humanism, which was based on a rediscovery of the ancient Greco-Latin achievements in science and the arts. The printing revolution became an invincible weapon for them. It led to freedom of the intellect from the regimentation of religious dogma and shaped modern European civilization.

Greek typography was quickly developed in the West so that scholars could read ancient texts in the original. This meant that the first books to be printed entirely in Greek were Greek Grammars. However, these were soon followed by the texts of Homer, Plato, Aristotle, Euclid, Pindar, Euripides, and so on.

By the end of the 15th c., Aldus Manutius had become the most influential publisher in Venice. He and a team of dedicated Greek scholars achieved something astonishing - the first printed editions of all the Greek classical texts. And his decision to employ the hundreds of letter combinations of the Byzantine hand greatly influenced the way Greek type design developed in the following centuries. He also reinstated the regular use of capital letters in Greek and Latin printed books.

When France became a dominant force in 16th century Europe, King François I wanted to surpass the intellectual glory of Florence and Venice. He ordered a new typeface to be created for his ambitious publishing program of the Greek classics. It was modelled on the handwriting of Angelos Vergikios, a famous Cretan calligrapher, and made use of the unsurpassed type-cutting skills of Claude Garamond. This resulted in the famous Grecs du roi characters, whose beauty and complex ligatures were greatly admired in the renowned Greek editions of Robert Estienne. They dominated Greek type design in European publishing for two centuries.

The 18th century was the age of the Enlightenment and printing played a major role in its dissemination. This era was also significant for Greek type design, because it saw a departure from the hundreds of ligatured lower-case letters towards simpler forms. At first, alternative characters remained for β, γ, θ, π, σ and τ, but today only the Byzantine c has survived in two forms: the initial/medial σ and the finial ς.

The early 19th century brought forth three new Greek typefaces in France, England and Germany. They were used in many editions, reflecting a renewed desire in Europe to study the Classics and publish the excavations of the antiquities in Greece.

After the successful Greek Revolution against the Ottoman Empire (1821–1827), printing quickly took off in the new independent Greek kingdom. Type was imported from European foundries, and Didot's Greek upright design was the unrivaled favorite. The cursive Greek type from Leipzig was only used in classical texts or as an italic substitute until an upright version appeared and challenged Didot's supremacy by the end of the 19th century.

From the early 1900s, the new Linotype and Monotype typesetting machines included the old Greek fonts in their catalogs. Monotype introduced some new designs, the most successful being Victor Scholderer's New Hellenic in 1927, and Gill Sans Greek after World War II.

During the interwar period, Greek type foundries grew considerably, and Em. Karpathakis' company was able to compete with German and French imports by introducing its own modernist sans serif, Olympia. After WWII, the Greek foundries PAP and Victoria competed with new designs until the introduction of photo-typesetting technology. In the 1970s, most European and American companies reacted to Greek publishers' demands by copying many successful Latin designs into the Greek alphabet. The market was inundated with typefaces like Helvetica Greek, Baskerville Greek, Univers Greek, Souvenir Greek, etc.

The digital revolution has made it possible to create new typefaces without huge investments. And while new type designers have re-evaluated the use of traditional and post-modern tendencies, the older designs still remain present in many publications.[19]

ΑΒΓΔΕΖΗΘΙΚΛΜΝΞΟΠΡΣΤΥΦΧΨΩ
ἀβϛγδὲζἦϑθῒκλμνξὄπρϛϲτῦφϕχψῷ

1756, Homer Greek — Robert & Andrew Foulis / Alexander Wilson

ΑΒΓΔΕΖΗΘΙΚΛΜΝΞΟΠΡΣΤΥΦΧΨΩ
ἄβϛγδὲζὴἦϑθῒκλμνξὄπρϲϛτῦφχψῷ

1804, Greek — Firmin Didot (Paris)

ΑΒΓΔΕΖΗΘΙΚΛΜΝΞΟΠΡΣΤΥΦΧΨΩ
ἄβγδὲζῆθῒκλμνξὄπρϲϛτῦφχψῷ

1809, Greek — Richard Porson (Cambridge)

ΑΒΓΔΕΖΗΘΙΚΛΜΝΞΟΠΡΣΤΥΦΧΨΩΩ
ἀβγδὲζῆθῒκλμνξὄπρϲϛτῦφχψῷ

1809, Greek — Karl Tauchnitz (Leipzig)

ΑΒΓΔΕΖΗΘΙΚΛΜΝΞΟΠΡΣΤΥΦΧΨΩ
ἀβγδέζῆθῒκλμνξὸπρϱϲϛτῦφχψῷ

1890s, Greek — Schelter & Giesecke A.G. (Leipzig)

ΑΒΓΔΕΖΗΘΙΚΛΜΝΞΟΠΡΣΤΥΦΧΨΩ
ἄβγδὲζῆθῒκλμνξὄπρϲϛτῦφχψῷ

1927, Greek 192 — New Hellenic — Victor Scholderer (Monotype)

ΑΒΓΔΕΖΗΘΪΚΛΜΝΞΟΠΡΣΤΥΦΧΨΩ
ἄβγδέζῆθῒκλμνξόπρϲϛτῦφχψώ

1936, Greek 572 — Gill Sans (Monotype)

ΑΒΓΔΕΖΗΘΙΚΛΜΝΞΟΠΡΣΤΥΦΧΨΩ
ἄβγδέζῆθικλμνξὄπρϲϛτῦφχψῷ

1937, Olympia Greek — Em. Karpathakis foundry (Athens)

ΑΒΓΔΕΖΗΘΙΚΛΜΝΞΟΠΡΣΤΥΦΧΨΩ
ἀβγδέζῆθῒκλμνξόπρϲϛτύφχψώ

1972, Helvetica Greek — Matthew Carter (Linotype)

Typical organization: Joshua Olsthoorn and Kostas Vlachakis, Greece
Typical organization, headquartered in Athens, Greece, was established in 2013 by
Kostas Vlachakis, born in Greece, and Joshua Olsthoorn, born in the Netherlands, each
in 1981. Their style is not mainstream, nor does it add new veneer to existing trends.
Instead, they see their work as an etymological process, to research the origins of form
and meaning, and transform the results into unique, typographic, visual concepts.
They've received many prizes, including one for the font design of the Greek Pavillion
entry at the Architecture Biennial in Venice, in 2018.

The works of this intercultural team are not necessarily pleasing or easily accessible.
Typical Organization consciously wants to stimulate debate, primarily through typographic
means. In the spirit of the Bauhaus and its successors, their visual language is limited to
what they consider essential, without stylistic differences between the Latin and Greek
fonts. Both are perfectly coordinated in their respective media.

3.28 Event poster, 2018

3.29 Poster for a mixed-media installation, 2015

3.30 Magazine cover, 2015

The Work on — off Mechanics in the Age on — off Art repro- duction.

de απο in
du βιο
μη stria
χανο liza
ποιη ti
on ση

Law III — To every action there is always opposed an equal reaction; or the mutual actions of two bodies upon each other are always equal, and directed to contrary parts.
— Isaac Newton

Νόμος ΙΙΙ — Στο ζεύγος των δυνάμεων στο οποίο οι δυνάμεις είναι ίσου μέτρου, αντίθετης κατεύθυνσης και ασκούνται σε διαφορετικό σώμα, ονομάζονται δράση-αντίδραση.
— Isaac Newton

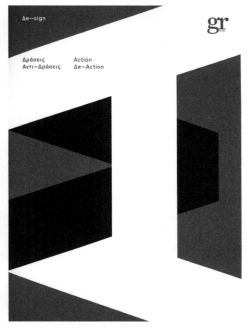

Δε—sign

gr

Δράσεις Action
Αντι—Δράσεις Δε—Action

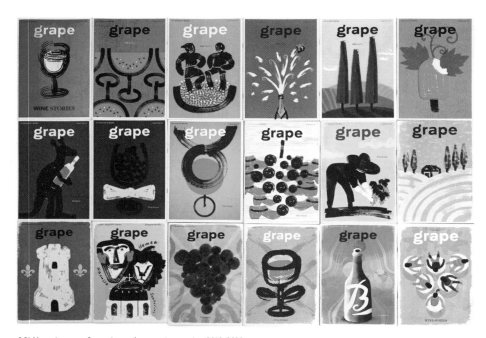

3.31 Magazine cover for a wine and gourmet magazine, 2016–2020

k2design, Greece

Yannis Kouroudis opened "Kouroudis Design" in Athens, Greece, in 1998. After new members joined, the company changed its name to "k2design", in 2002. Today, k2design includes Kouroudis' son, Menelaos, and a team of specialists and external employees. k2design offers complete solutions for branding, corporate identity, product communications and packaging. K2design is one of the most highly commended Greek graphic design firms. The company has received awards, prizes, media coverage and additional accolades, both in Greece and abroad.

k2design focuses on packaging design, often utilizing expressive and colorful illustrations. Typography serves a supporting role, resonating with the illustrative forms present in all facets of their design. Handwriting mixes with an antiqua and a grotesque without fear of contact.

Katerina Antonaki, Greece

Katerina Antonaki is a freelance graphic designer and researcher. She holds a PhD in the critical theory and practice of design from Goldsmiths University of London. Since 2013, she has been a guest lecturer in the Graphic Design department at the Technological Educational Institute of Athens. She has worked on countless interdisciplinary projects in the design and advertising industries. Her current focus is on the role of visual communication in establishing brand identity; visual identity in the public arena and spontaneity in the design process. She is enthusiastic about codes and the poetry of things.

Antonaki's work ranges from exuberant typographic experiments for the branding of a museum's cultural posters to playful, colorful posters for children. Antouki employs constructed grotesque typefaces, mostly set in capitals, and the most diverse handwriting.

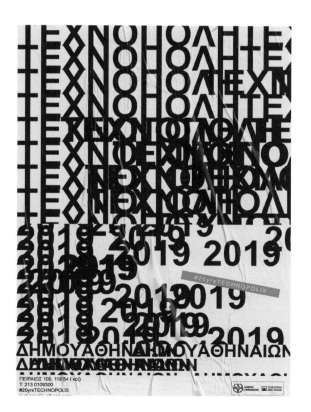

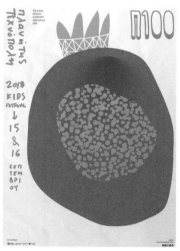

3.32 20 Anniversary of Museum Technopolis, 2019

3.33 Kids festival, 2018

MNP, Greece

Katerina Papanagiotou is the Creative Director and founding member of MNP, a creative studio based in Athens, Greece, since 2003. The six members of MNP specialize in communications design, packaging, website design, and publishing. The daily life of Greek culture inspires their creative output in a rather liberated way.

Both poster series shown are characterized by a sequential design approach, with informative text deliberately pushed to the margins in each. In the first series, powerful display letters in gray, yellow, and green are superimposed in a manner reminiscent of letterpress printing. Legibility recedes into the background and type becomes image.

Questions like "Would you dare?" literally jump out at us in the second series, where they sometimes slant left and other times to the right. Typographic conventions – where it's taboo for an italic to lean left – are broken! The small line spacing of the bold, upright, Greek headline adds appropriate extra weight and pressure.

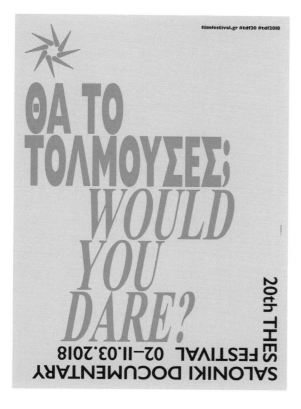

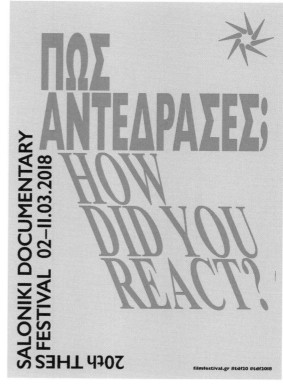

3.34 Posters for an event series, 2016 and 2017

3.35 Poster series for a movie festival, 2018

Zhiqian Li

Studied Industry Design at College of Architecture and
Urban Planning, Tongji University, Shanghai
Co-founder of 3type, Initiator and project lead of Shanghai
Type and Type Tour
Since 2017 Distinguished Research Fellow at Type Lab,
Shanghai Academy of Fine Arts
Since 2017 scholar at Type Lab, Shanghai Academy of Fine Arts
Author: Stories of Western Typefaces (西文字体的故事),
2013 (no English Version)

A brief history of Hanzi

Chinese characters, or Hanzi, originated in China.
The earliest Hanzi, oracle bone script, was found
on animal bones or tortoise shells in 1300 BCE.
Not until Li Shu, or Clerical Script, emerged did
Hanzi come to have a stable fundamental form
similar to what we see today. Throughout history,
Hanzi has developed many writing styles. But not
only the writing styles have changed over time,
the characters in use have also varied. New Hanzi
were invented, while old Hanzi were given new
a pronunciation or different meanings from time
to time. As there are diverse ways in which Hanzi
can be written, this led to the development of
diverse forms. The more recent Simplified Chinese
Movement created a large amount of new glyphs
for existing Hanzi characters.

鸡蛋 —— 鸡旦　　　愛 —— 爱
停车 —— 仃车　　　葉 —— 叶
快餐 —— 快夕　　　進 —— 进
二简字　　　　　　简化字

圕 —— 图书馆（书在房子里）
啤 —— 口字旁+卑（beer，表音）
民国时期新造字

3.36 Second round of simplified Chinese characters

Logogram

Hanzi is the most-used ideographic and logographic script in the world. An ideogram/logogram may have multiple meanings and pronunciations, and users can create new Hanzi or merge existing Hanzi to express new meanings.

all Hanzi characters were squeezed into the same type size. This had a profound influence both on the design of Hanzi and on how it was set. A group of squared Hanzi was easily able to meet the requirements of both vertical and horizontal setting, and this tradition has survived into today's digital age.

米 料 粨 粁 糎

3.37 1 meter, 10 meters, 100 meters, 1 kilometer, 10 kilometers

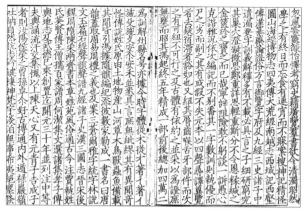

3.38 Guangyun, Southern Song Dynasty (1169), wood block printing

Users of Hanzi

From past to present, Hanzi has been used as a script in many languages, not just in Chinese. Hanzi was and still is used as a part of the writing systems in Japan, Korea, Vietnam and Singapore. Over history, some neighboring states adopted the characteristics of Hanzi and developed their own Hanzi-derived scripts, e.g. Sawndip (状字) and Tangut (西夏文). Some researchers even tried to adapt Hanzi into their own writing system.

Writing direction

Since its emergence in 1400 BCE, Hanzi was written vertically. And when it was cut in wood blocks and printed on paper in the 8th century, it was set vertically. In fact, Hanzi was written and read in the vertical direction for a very long time. Then, about 100 years ago, the Chinese started to write, set and read Chinese horizontally. In the late 19th century, Gutenberg's printing was introduced to China by missionaries. For the sake of convenience, in type production and setting

History

The history of Chinese type design is short. From 1960, the Shanghai Printing Institute recruited a team of people from different backgrounds, such as type engravers, calligraphers and lettering artists, who later became known as type designers. Before that, Hanzi was written and engraved in a tradition that was distinctly based on calligraphy (which is executed without the deliberate consciousness of the designer).

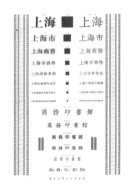

3.39 Fangsong, the style imitating Songti

3.40 Type specimen from The Commercial Press, 1919

3.41 Different type sizes of Kaiti (the standard writing style)

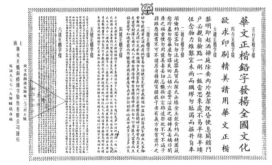

3.42 40-50s type specimen from Shanghai, Hanzi in traditional Chinese glyphs

3.43 Four important fonts, produced by Shanghai Printing Institute of Technology

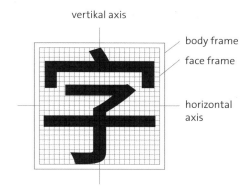

vertikal axis

body frame

face frame

horizontal axis

3.44 Measurement and geometric principles of Hanzi

Hanzi metrics

Today's Hanzi design still follows the rules that were established in the age of metal type. The majority of Chinese type designers do not strictly follow a decided set of metrics but rather tend to rely heavily on experience. The existing metrics appear vague, inconsistent, and sometimes un-measurable. The figure below shows two groups of Hanzi metrics that have been well-received. However, there are other metrics that are more complicated and controversial.

Body frame & face frame

Body frame refers to the full surface of a type. Face frame refers to the area where the strokes are placed, namely, where the "typeface" itself is located. These frames are usually square, but rectangles with other proportions are also possible.

Axes

In the days of metal type, Chinese type designers drew their design on paper with grids on it. A cross was positioned at the center of the frame. By using these two crossing lines as guidelines, type designers managed their design within the frame. Vertical and horizontal axes look stable in the frame. But if we think out of the box, they are movable as well.

Optical adjustment

Like other scripts, optical adjustment is essential when designing Hanzi as well. The contour and the blackness of Hanzi vary depending on its cons-truction and stroke numbers. Type designers need to do a lot of work on strokes and take care with the negative space to arrive at a balanced look for all of the Hanzi in a font.

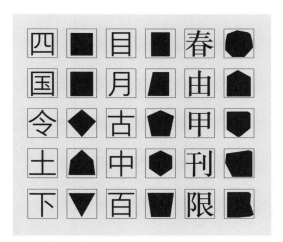

3.45 Outer forms of Hanzi

Style matching

Songti (called Mincho in Japan) is a style inspired by woodblock printing derived from the late Song to Ming Dynasty (12th–17th century) in China. Modern Songti (Mincho) takes inspiration from Latin serif type style as well, meaning that they are usually put together. Heiti is a type style that was invented by the Japanese (called Gothic in Japan) and brought to China. It is directly inspired by the sans serif style of the Latin alphabet. Aside from these two main styles, there are another two widely used styles: Kaiti and Fangsong. Kaiti is a calligraphy style that has been considered standard for a long time. Fangsong means 'imitating Song', and is another style inspired by the Song Dynasty. The difference between Fangsong & Songti is the object they aim to imitate, the former being early Song (10th–12th), while the latter is late Song and Ming. Kaiti & Fangsong are sometimes used to match Italic styles or some calligraphic styles. A non-visual matching strategy, for example, having a Kaiti and a sans serif together, can also be widely seen. Countless examples of mixed style matching can be found in old movies, old printed matters and street signs in old towns.

3.46 Style matching with the Latin alphabet

3.47 Height matching with the letters of the Latin Alphabet

Height matching

Unlike the letters of the Latin alphabet, Hanzi does not have a baseline to stand on. When matching with Latin, Cyrillic, Greek or other letters and numerals, the position of the Hanzi body frame becomes a problem.

A flexible strategy should be adopted depending on the individual situation: lowercase with Hanzi, capital letters with Hanzi, small and capital letters with Hanzi, small letters with few descenders with Hanzi, small caps letters with Hanzi, and so on.

Size matching

When Hanzi and Latin letters are set together, their relative sizes are different in different situations. In some multi-script typeface families, we might find that the Latin counterpart has to be enlarged to match Hanzi.

3.49 The Chinese-English translation of the "Golden Needle", 1919

3.48 Dictionary of the Chinese Language, Part I, Robert Morrison, 1823

Future development of Hanzi design

An increasing number of young people have been becoming involved in Hanzi design in recent years. And, in the meantime, the market for typeface has reached a historical high in China. New type design tools like Glyphs have paved the way for amateurs who want to make a Hanzi font by their own. And the number of type design courses being offered in the countries of East Asia is on the rise. The design theory of Hanzi is evolving, and many European and American type designers have managed to design in Greek, Cyrillic, Arabic, Armenian, even Devanagari and Hangul. I believe that, very soon, they will also be designing Hanzi.[20]

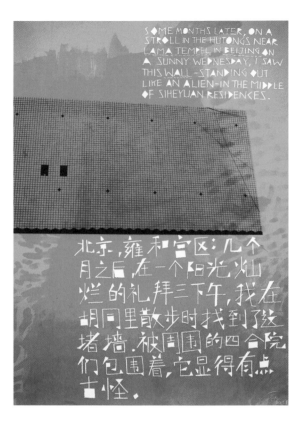

3.50 Poster using the font Bojing, "When a Stairway Meets a Wall", 2013

Yi Meng Wu, China

Yi Meng Wu was born in 1983 in Shanghai and is a visual designer, artist and cultural interpreter. She grew up in China and Germany and lives in Berlin. Wu studied Visual Communication in Essen, Berlin and Paris. Her Berlin studio "Wu 無" is a place where handicraft and sensuality are very much alive in an otherwise digitally dominated world. She offers lectures and workshops and teaches at universities and other institutions on topics ranging from intercultural design and typography to urban artistic findings.

The designer was inspired by the geometric approach of Bauhaus, prompting a shared stylistic affinity between the Latin and Chinese fonts of poster, which was designed for a 2013 Shanghai Poster Biennale on the theme "Discover". Later, a type foundry commissioned Wu to develop the typeface.

Hongjie Guan, China

Hong Jie Guan was born in 1992 and is an art director. He is a former member of the China Designers' Association and was a finalist in "The 6th Founder Award Chinese Font Design Competition".

Illustrated pictorial motifs interact here with the Chinese characters, which are elegant, curved and have a high stroke contrast. They are reminiscent of a time when Hanzi was still cut and printed in wooden blocks. In contrast, the Latin font, a sans-serif, is set in bold, constructed capitals.

3.51 "All embracing" animal alphabet, 2020

Yan Song Li, China

Yan Song Li founded his 10⁵ LIGHT-YEARS design studio in 2019. He is a graduate of the Inner Mongolia Normal University and has been involved in visual design since 2001. In addition to his commercial design business, he conducts research into the graphic reconstruction of Chinese characters and traditional Chinese culture.

The negative type seems to dissolve into nothingness and is difficult to read. The characters have strong size contrasts, are symmetrical, and have been distorted to appear spatial. The writing is vertical from top to bottom, and then continues in the columns from right to left.

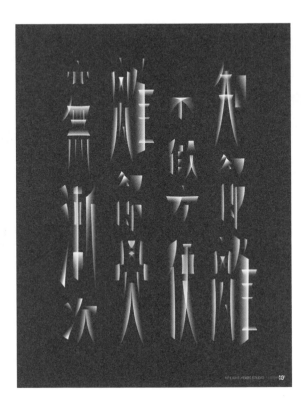

3.52 Illusion of light and shadow, 2017

3.53 Font Hui Song, demonstration poster, 2020

Hai Long Xiang, China

Hai Long Xiang is a graphic designer specializing in branding, typography and packaging design. He lives in Shanghai. He has won design prizes such as Pentawards, the IF Design Award and the Gold Pin Design Award.

The typeface Hui Song reinterprets the classical Songti script, comparable to the Latin Classical Antiqua. It spread during the Song Dynasty (960 to 1279 CE) when woodblock printing was at its peak. The monochrome representation of the landscape and the red stamp in the right margin address the spiritual and intellectual elite of a tradition-conscious China.

Haytham Nawar

Arabic script and typography

Arabic is a Semitic language that first emerged between the first and fourth centuries CE. Arabic has 28 basic letters, eight of which can only be differentiated by diacritics. In older spelling, the diacritics were used less, but they were then added to facilitate Qur'an recitation. The direction of writing in Arabic is from right to left, and letters have different forms that change depending on their position in a word. The four positions (initial, medial, final, and isolated) are presented as actual forms, and this results in each word being a set of mostly connected groups of letters.

Character	Initial	Medium	Final	Isolated	Character	Initial	Medium	Final	Isolated
Alif	ا	ل	ل	ا	Taa'	ط	ط	ط	ط
Ba'	ب	ب	ب	ب	Za'	ظ	ظ	ظ	ظ
Ta'	ت	ت	ت	ت	'ayn	ع	ع	ع	ع
Tha'	ث	ث	ث	ث	Ghayn	غ	غ	غ	غ
Jim	ج	ج	ج	ج	Fa'	ف	ف	ف	ف
Ha'	ح	ح	ح	ح	Qaf	ق	ق	ق	ق
Kha'	خ	خ	خ	خ	Kaf	ك	ك	ك	ك
Dal	د	د	د	د	Lam	ل	ل	ل	ل
Dhal	ذ	ذ	ذ	ذ	Mim	م	م	م	م
Ra'	ر	ر	ر	ر	Nun	ن	ن	ن	ن
Zayn	ز	ز	ز	ز	Ha'	ه	ه	ه	ه
Sin	س	س	س	س	Waw	و	و	و	و
Shin	ش	ش	ش	ش	Ya	ي	ي	ي	ي
Sad	ص	ص	ص	ص	Hamza			ء	ء
Dad	ض	ض	ض	ض	Ta' marbuta			ة	ة

3.54 Arabic letters and their different forms

Arabic calligraphic rules did not consider potential analytical letter permutations that would be useful for typesetters and modern fonts. To write in Arabic, one must understand its structure as it is not a simple line-up of letters as in the Latin script. Letters in Arabic are connected, and these connections cannot be understood outside of their context. Since some letters use similar strokes, a sequence of letters can easily be misread for another sequence. One of the consecutive letters can have either a dissimilar stroke or a dissimilar horizontally stretched connection in such cases.

Arabic typography started at the beginning of the sixteenth century as a by-product of Latin typesetters. To date, font technology has not yet wholly solved this wide range of flexibility, which is a design feature in the Arabic script and one of the essential reading aids. There have been attempts at simplification of Arabic by typesetters. Although all problems that arise from converting Arabic to a font would disappear if given a similar structure to that of Latin script, this approach would render Arabic illegible and culturally strange.

When talking about Arabic writing culture, traditional calligraphy is aesthetically skilled writing in an identifiable Islamic script or style (e.g. Kufic, Naskh, Thuluth, Diwani, Ruqaa, etc.). In contrast with the five vertical levels of reference (i.e., baseline, x-height, ascender, descender, and caps-height) in Latin script, Arabic script possesses more invisible typographic levels. A typeface could use up to twelve imaginary

3.55 Original form and derivative forms obtained by uninterrupted cursive movement

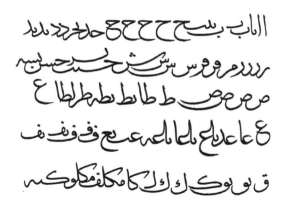

3.56 The shapes of letters multiplied as they were adapted to each new configuration according to the calligrapher's skill and imagination.

3.57 Graceful Ottoman diwani calligraphy, Istanbul, nineteenth century

3.58 Persian Calligraphy in Nestaliq Script, nineteenth century

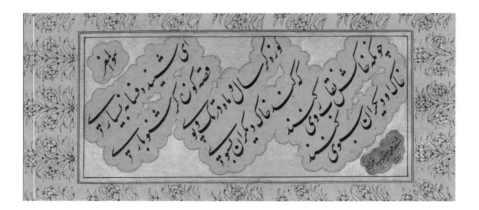

typographic levels, depending on the Arabic style that the typeface is to be based on. Hence, Arabic type designers must be acquainted with Arabic calligraphic styles and systems. The Arabic script is subject to a rule system called script grammar. One of its aspects results in a script that supports more text in a line but fewer lines on a page. As Arabic script necessitates generous line spacing, typographers who work with Latin script find it particularly challenging to create bi-scriptural designs with parallel texts.

In the tenth century, calligrapher Ibn Muqla normalized the principles for drawing Arabic letters for the first time. He proposed rules that are relevant to traditional calligraphy and modern typography globally. Each Arabic calligraphic style is ruled by several guides or systems (i.e., dot, circle, and similarity), which dictate the letters' proportions. Accordingly, the Arabic type anatomy is in the hands of the type of designer based on the calligraphic style that will serve as a base. In an attempt to allocate typographic terms to Arabic type and typography, Pascal El Zoghbi explains: "Instead of one mean-line – in Latin typefaces, the x-height – there may be several: tooth-, loop-, and eye-heights. Instead of a single ascender, there may be two, called the 'Sky.' In place of a single descender, there may be two or three, called the 'Earth'. Two further invisible lines define the baseline's position and thickness."

3.59 Different kufic styles

Early kufic

Eastern kufic

Foliate kufic

Knotted kufic

Square kufic

Several attempts have been made throughout history to try to modernize the Arabic letters and their typographical styles, but to no avail. Moreover, several endeavors have been made to simplify the Arabic script and solve the problem of adapting it to new technologies, such as Nasri Khattar's project "Unified Arabic", which was presented to and rejected by the Academy of the Arabic Language in Cairo in 1958. Previously in the same decade, Mahmoud Taymour's project "The Initial Form of the Letters" attempted to abbreviate the Arabic letters to a single form and was approved by the Academy of the Arabic Language in Cairo but with no further expansion. Ahmed Lakhdar Ghazal made other efforts with his project "ASV Codar", a script reform similar to Khattar's unified Arabic letters form. In 1958,

سن | Tooth   نقطة | Diacritic Dot   Sky 1
سماء ١   Ascender Sky 2
سماء ٢
عين - حلقة - سن ١   X-Height Loop-/Eye-Height 1
عين - حلقة - سن ٢   Loop-/Eye-Height 2
سن ٣   Tooth-Height 3
سن ٤   Tooth-Height 4
سن ٥   Tooth-Height 5
سمك القاعدة   BaseThickness
قاعدة   Baseline Base
Whiteness / Space بياض / فضاء
أرض ١   Earth 1
أرض ٢   Earth 2
كاسة | Bowl   لوزة / عين | Almond / Eye

3.60 "Anatomy Arabic style: from earth to sky", 2015

this system too failed to receive the approval of the Academy of the Arabic Language in Cairo. However, Linotype recognized it and successfully distributed it. In addition to these projects, Roberto Hamm addressed the same subject when, in 1975, he completed a constructed Arabic typeface for the Algerian Arabization Institute. Lastly, Sabry Hegazy's method, also based on simplifying the way, consisted of Arabic letters written to achieve better legibility. He created a set of thirty-seven independent letters and ten diacritic marks, which unfortunately did not make any noticeable impact.

In the contemporary practice of Arabic typography and Arabic Type design, there are ongoing debates about respect for the script's characteristics and its calligraphic traditions and the idea of "modernizing" or latinizing it to match the Latin script terms of typography and type design. Linguist and scholar Thomas Milo explains, "there is a gap between Arabic calligraphy and Arabic type because of the lack of understanding of traditional rules." In fact, available sources that try to tackle this issue only touch upon the calligraphic standardization of isolated letters by Ibn Muqla. However, this standardization does not consider the flexibility of the Arabic script and is not relevant to the connected letters.

A general rejection of experimentation has hindered the progress of the Arabic type. Designer and scholar Huda Smitshuijzen AbiFarès argues in favor of Arabic and Latin matchmaking. It has become easier to produce and publish a font, especially with the growth of the Internet. This is resulting in a remarkable amount of activity (still in its infancy) in the field of ty-

3.61 Following Ibn Muqla's principles, the proportions begin from a circle in thuluth script, tenth century

pographic experimentation and design and a general movement towards the creation of international font families to cater to today's communication needs. "Designing digital Arabic fonts that can be used in multi-scriptural design in a global context is the best way to keep the Arabic script alive," AbiFarès said.

The challenge for Arabic type designers stems from the religious role that Arabic script has assumed in the Arab/Muslim world. This started when reading and writing were mentioned in the Qur'an as a medium for transmitting the words of God. The religious attitude vis-a-vis the Arabic script considered any deviation from tradition to be a disfigurement of the script. Although Arabic calligraphy remains one of the most expressive and beautiful traditions, Arabic type still needs to evolve to unfold its full potential.[21]

Golnar Kat Rahmani, Iran

Golnar Kat is a graphic designer from Iran. She is one of the co-founders of the Studios "Katrahmani" in Berlin. The design agency started up in 2016 and specializes in communication design and consulting services in the areas of typography, font design, visual identity and editorial design. Her work focuses on Persian and Arabic typography.

Type is used here primarily as a decorative element, a motif typical of Persian typography. On the magazine cover, the characters morph into new formal units, become blurred at the edges, almost dissolve, and leave a ghostly impression.

The poster shows an angular black shape in the background, which could be a carpet on which the announcement of the festival is presented. The font extends over the edge, taking up space.

3.62 Design of a magazine cover, 2018

3.63 KT Poster, 2018

EASTERN & WESTERN **ARABIC** NUMERALS

3.64 "Happiness in Words", typographical design as a basis for an animation, 2020

3.65 Eastern & Western Arabic Numerals, 2021

Nada Abdallah, Lebanon

Nada Abdallah is an artist, designer, educator and the founder of the Bilarabic Design Festival. She studied Visual Communication at the American University of Sharjah and at Lebanese University. Prior to joining the University of Sharjah, she taught Design at the Higher Colleges of Technology, Lebanese University and Lebanese International University. She has won several awards in design and photography, in the USA and elsewhere. Active since the early 1990s, her work and her research focus on Arabic Calligraphy and Typography, and prehistoric motif design.

Both designs feature highly geometricized characters. The font composition against the blue sky is reminiscent of wall mosaics. Fine lines alternate with triangles and the so-called diacritical dots of the Arabic script are represented as small triangles.

3.66 Self-initiated program: Sporadic schooling, 2020

3.67 The moving poster, 2019

Engy Aly, Egypt

Engy Aly was born in 1982 in Cairo and later went on to study Graphic
Design in her hometown. Afterwards, she worked for the Cairo design studio
"fileclub" before establishing herself as an independent designer in 2009.
Her commissions focus on cultural projects and her personal work explores
the nebulous boundary between art and design. In 2013, she obtained an
MFA from the Academy of Art and Design in Basel.

*The typeface used at "Heliopolis" features a tremendous stroke contrast and is
inspired by the Egyptian store signs of the 80s.*

*The "Moving Poster" was created for an exhibition of more than 100 animated
displays. The background is an abstracted map showing the streets and places
around the exhibition location.*

*In the "Sporadic Schooling" poster, the individual characters and glyphs are
based on the same geometric construction. Their positioning, which seems
random, is deliberate used. The color palette of both posters is reduced
and primary and secondary colors dominate.*

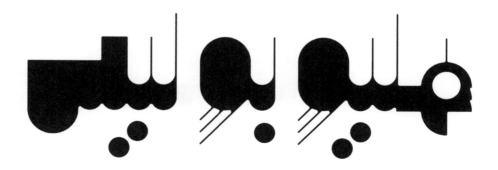

3.68 Heliopolis, typographic experiment, 2016

3.69 Khotout West Elbalad Research, Design Supervision
J. Walter Thompson, Al-Ismaelia Real Estate Investment, Cairo, 2016

Please describe your educational background, including your studies, work/study, and travel.

My undergrad major was printmaking at Helwan University in Cairo, where I got my MFA in New Media Arts. My second Master's in Spatial Design was at Zurich University of the Arts, then I did my Ph.D. at Plymouth University in the UK.

What countries or cultures have you worked and/or lived in/with extensively or closely? Have you had formative experiences in other cultures?

As an Egyptian, I have lived and worked in many cities in Egypt including the gigantic Cairo and the cosmopolitan Alexandria. I travel a lot to study, teach, give talks, workshops, events, etc. I don't often stay for long in one place – it depends on my reason for traveling.

Two Fulbright grants took me to the US to study. The first time in New York, affiliated to the School of Visual Arts in NY, and the second time in LA, affiliated to University of California. I see Egypt as a multilayered country: African, Arabic-speaking, Coptic before Muslim, and Mediterranean. All reflected in the many layers of cultural diversity. In Europe, I lived among Switzerland's multilingual communities where at least two of the following languages were spoken: German, French, Italian, and Romany. The US is a cultural melting pot with extreme diversity and very different cultures. Before returning to Egypt, I was in Hong Kong, a richly multicultural island that has gone from British to Chinese rule. Living and working in Greece felt closest to home for me, confirming my belief in a Mediterranean culture.

I have recently focused more on research on the African continent, and I am attempting to write an African narrative of the continent's design history.

What did you know about these countries/cultures before you started working together?

As a scholar research is my job. I had a mainly Eurocentric education, so I like to explore places with cultures very different to that. Before traveling, I learn about a place and its culture, only to discover you learn most by interacting with local people. I am

Haytham Nawar
Studied at Faculty of Fine Arts, Helwan University, Cairo, Egypt and at the Institute of Design & Technology, Zurich University of the Arts, Switzerland Ph.D. from Plymouth University, UK
Since 2016 Professor at the Department of the Arts, The American University in Cairo Teaching and work experience in the USA, Hong Kong, Switzerland, Greece and more Co-author with Bahia Shehab: A History of Arab Graphic Design (2020)

inquisitive about the human element and the social aspect of traveling. What really matters cannot be learned from a distance, it's all about interaction and cultural exchange.

What specific differences have you noticed in how students learn in other countries/cultures?

Students behave differently in different cultures, but individuals still count, of course, and every student is unique. The education system and society definitely play a significant role in the classroom.

Students are shy in some cultures and need encouragement to be more proactive. In other cultures, students suffer from a lack of diversity, so you need to increase their awareness. Educators must adapt and invent their own teaching methods and tools to overcome differences.

Teaching or working in a culture different from your own involves adapting to different social and moral norms, including issues of class and gender. What has your experience been like in these areas, and in what ways did you adapt your working or teaching methods as a result?

Different cultures deal differently with global issues like race, gender, etc. You need to learn and understand each culture to communicate better with your students. Respecting differences, finding similarities, and trying to bridge between cultures helps. A common language makes things more comfortable, and design is a universal language. Take body language, for example. I move my hands a lot while explaining. Teaching in Hong Kong showed me this is a Mediterranean habit and distracting for students there. So, I had to adapt by reducing my gestures.

What are the benefits you have gained from teaching in countries/cultures that are different from own culture?

Working with different cultures can be challenging, but I believe the benefits outweigh. Interacting promotes intercultural understanding, expands awareness and enables a more creative environment. Mixing cultures leads to new solutions by testing visual communication more efficiently and inventing more universal and adaptive designs. I like my students to create multi-scriptual designs, even with languages they don't understand. It's fascinating to see people dealing with a language from a purely visual perspective. Teaching abroad motivated me in my own scholarly work. I once taught Graphic Design History (Eurocentric) while my colleague taught Asian Design History. Learning about Asian design history made me want to record Arab design history. The result was my first textbook History of Arab Graphic Design co-authored by Bahia Shehab.

3.70 Khotout West Elbalad Research, Design Supervision
J. Walter Thompson, Al-Ismaelia Real Estate Investment, Cairo, 2016

4.01 The object color depends on the light source.

COLOR

Hardly any of the means used in design give rise to as many complex and emotional associations as color does. Like listening to music, we react sub-consciously and spontaneously to color with feelings such as enthusiasm, rejection or disinterest. If a person is interested in pursuing the matter further or has musical training, the emotional first impression can be followed up by a cognitive analysis of aspects such as harmonies, the beat, rhythm and tone. Our perception of color can be just as multi-layered. One goal of designers is to not only be guided by their gut feeling when choosing a color, but also make use of tried and tested decision-making criteria. Culturally anchored color harmonies, color contrasts, as well as physical and chemical properties should also be included in design decisions.

Color is defined in different ways depending on the specific field being applied:
1. Physics: electromagnetic spectrum
2. Chemistry: molecular structure
3. Physiology: physical sensations
4. Symbolism: cultural and historical meaning
5. Psychology: sensual perception and processing
6. Image reproduction: the reproduction medium
7. Art: socio-individual criteria
8. Design: targeted communication

All of these areas are relevant for designers. Physics explains how colors come to exist, while chemistry deals with the molecular property of the surface and the resulting color effects like matt or glossy. Physiology studies our physical and emotional reactions to colors, which particularly plays a role in color schemes used in public and private spaces, in hospitals for instance. Color symbolism/semantics are anchored in culture and will be looked at in more detail below. The psychology of perception describes phenomena like optical illusions. In image production, a difference is made between color reproduction, above all when images are printed, published on the Web, or on electronic devices, etc. Art provides us with new impulses and expands our horizon. Only when we take all of these areas into consideration can we manage to communicate in a targeted manner through our design work.

Basically, the ability to perceive of color depends on light. At twilight we can still distinguish between light and dark, but can hardly differentiate colors. It is only in daylight or under artificial light that we can identify what color objects are. The light rays enter the eye and are transferred into nerve impulses with the help of color receptors that react to very specific wavelengths. This information is then transmitted to the brain. There are two different types of photoreceptor: rods and cones. The cones are responsible for how we perceive color and are divided into three types, each of which reacts to light in a certain wave range. That is why they are called red, green and blue receptors. The rods react to lightness and darkness and allow us to see in twilight or at night.

Since Isaac Newton's prism experiment, which showed how light was refracted in a glass prism, we know that light is a combination of spectral colors. When a rainbow occurs, what we are seeing is the sunlight being refracted in raindrops, which shows us the colors red, orange, yellow, green, blue and violet. If this is done the other way round, and all of the colors of the spectrum are brought together, for example through a converging lens, the result is so-called "white" light. When we mix different source colors, this is called additive color mixing, as it always results in a brighter light. All other source colors are mixed using the primary colors red, green and blue. If you mix the source colors red and green, this results in the secondary color yellow.

When so-called white light, which contains the entire spectrum of spectral colors, hits an object, certain colors are absorbed while others are reflected. This can be demonstrated taking a yellow banana as an example. If white light hits the banana, blue is absorbed while red and green are reflected. This has to do with the molecular state of the banana's surface, which can of course change, for example when the banana is overly ripe and therefore no longer appears to be a shining yellow, but more of a brownish-yellow color. The banana only appears yellow to us because our optic nerves interpret electromagnetic waves in a particular way.

We therefore have source colors and material colors, which are also referred to as object colors. One essential difference between the two is the way in which they mix. With source colors, we talk about additive color mixing. When the object colors are mixed, it is called subtractive color mixing, because individual wavelengths are subtracted or absorbed and the color therefore becomes increasingly darker. If all source colors are absorbed, then what we see is black. We are familiar with mixing object colors in our everyday lives, but not with additive color mixing. However, only when you are able to tell the difference, will you be able to understand why colors look different on a computer screen or a smartphone display to what is possible in print. Monitors work with source colors, while printing uses object colors. In the RGB system, about 16 million colors can be displayed. In offset printing with the basic colors cyan (C), magenta (M) and yellow (Y) and the additional so-called key color black (K=key), under optimum conditions approx. 500,000 color tones are possible, thus a great deal fewer.[1]

Color systems

Europe has experienced many ideas and systems of color theory from the Antique through the Renaissance and Enlightenment and right up to Bauhaus. Aristoteles assumed that all colors were a mixture of light and dark. Leonardo da Vinci dedicated himself above all to the color harmonies, and Isaac Newton made groundbreaking scientific discoveries, which were then questioned by Johann Wolfgang von Goethe. He and Philipp Otto Runge researched the symbolic and intellectual relationships between the colors. In the 20th century, a new discipline — psychology, and gestalt psychology in particular — provided new knowledge that explained perception. On the other hand, there also emerged rational methods reduced to mathematical laws, like those of the chem-

HOW THE OBJECT COLORS ARE FORMED

1. Light hits the object
2. Blue is absorbed
3. Green+red=yellow

4.02 Origin of the object colors

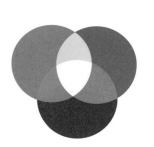

RGB
ADDITIVE COLOR SYSTEM

Primary colors: red / green / blue
Secondary colors:
yellow / magenta / cyan

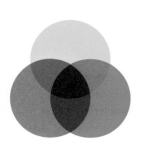
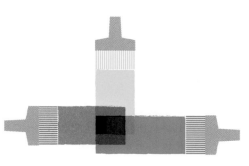

CMY(K)
SUBTRACTIVE COLOR SYSTEM

Primary colors:
cyan / magenta / yellow
Secondary colors: green / red / blue

K=key, the additional black key color that provides depth to the image and the deep grey and black in printing.

4.03 Mixing colors

ist Wilhelm Ostwald. And printing engineer Harald Küppers must also be mentioned. He developed a color wheel that was based on eight basic colors and was optimized for mixing object colors.

In China, color identification systems were closely linked with a mythology influenced through and through by shamanism and the veneration of the dead. Worshipping the heavens and astronomy also played a substantial role (approx. 5000 BC).[2] The sky was divided into the cyan-colored dragons in the east, the white tiger in the west, the red bird in the south, the black snake-necked turtle in the north and the yellow dragon in the middle. It was believed that all other colors originated from these five basic colors. These five colors were later found in Taoism (4th century BC) and in Chinese medicine, and in the theory of the five elements: green/blue stands for wood, red for fire, yellow for Earth, white for metal and black for water.[3] A century before that saw the emergence of Confucianism, the philosophy that greatly influenced many aspects of life in China for thousands of years, including state theory and political doctrine. It had a pragmatic, less metaphysical orientation and used the colors of clothing to define a person's rank in society.[4] Color was also used for accentuation in painting. More than anything else, color was handled with great care. Influenced by ink painting and also by woodcuts, the line played a considerably greater role than color. Unlike the western tradition, the idea was not to simulate nature, but rather to reproduce the mood and the resonance of the energy of the image (Qi Yun).[5] This approach, which was formulated by Xie He in the 6th century, is not that far removed from the ideas of abstract painting in western art.

Arab scientists like Abu Ali al-Hasan ibn al-Haitham (Latin name: Alhazen), already possessed innovative knowledge of the optics of the eye in the 9th century.[6] It was not until three centuries later that the results of this research reached Europe, where more philosophical notions were more common up until the Renaissance. A turning point came in the 17th century with Galileo Galilei, Johannes Kepler and others, followed by Newton's findings.

4.04 Painting of Flowers and Bird, Wen Shu, 1595 - 1634

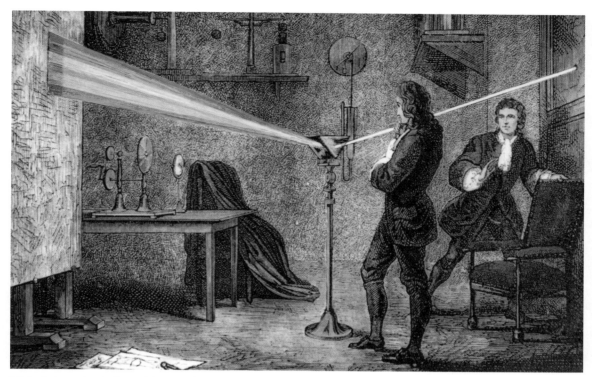

4.05 Newton's experiment refracting light using a glass prism

The following color systems are important nowadays:

A Device-independent
CIELAB color space (also L*a*b*)
International standard for all perceivable colors, reference color space
in color management

B Device-dependent (e.g., monitors, cameras, printers)
↗ RGB system
Additive mixing of the three primary source colors red, green and blue
↗ HSB system
    Hue = color tone (00 – 3600)
    Saturation = intensity, purity of the color tone
    (0% is gray, 100% is fully saturated)
    Brightness = whiteness or blackness (0% is black, 100% is white)
    Derived from the RGB system.
↗ CMYK system
    Standard system used in printing
↗ Special colors in printing: HKS and Pantone

Color wheels
There are many different color wheels and all of them aim to create
a system and offer design aids. Like the rainbow colors, most of them
are arranged according to their wavelength range, from yellow to orange,
red to blue, etc. In color theory, the color wheel by Bauhaus teacher
Johannes Itten is very widespread and is good for explaining color
contrasts. However, his primary colors red, blue and yellow do not work
in practice, and the resulting colors are dull when mixed. Harald Küpper's
color wheel is used here. It is based on the primary colors for printing.
It also has some disadvantages, for example, that the space between
yellow and the other colors is too big. It's all about finding the optimum
solution for each individual case. In painting, for example, you not only
need three basic colors in addition to black and white, but a minimum
of seven in order to mix all color tones.[7]

Primary colors: **Secondary colors:**
Cyan / Magenta / Yellow   Red Orange / Blue Violet / Green

Tertiary colors:
Yellow Orange / Red / Red Violet / Blue / Blue Green / Yellow Green

HUE (COLOR TONE)

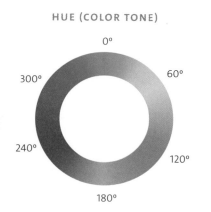

SATURATION

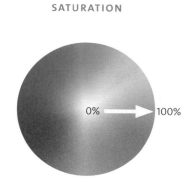

BRIGHTNESS

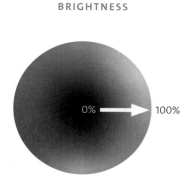

4.06 HSB system

PRIMARY COLORS

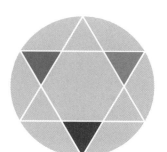

SECONDARY COLORS

TERTIARY COLORS

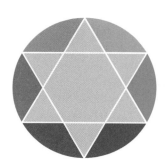

4.07 Küpper's color wheel

Color contrasts, color tones and color harmonies

Johannes Itten, as well as Josef Albers, played a
considerable role in spreading a knowledge-based
and analytical basic theory of color via the Bauhaus
pre-course initiated by Itten. Albers described color as
"one of the most relative means of artistic expression"
and proposed approaching the subject in teaching
through "inquisitive learning", so that one can, through
"trial and error", gain a sensitivity for color nuances,
brightness, harmonies and illusions.[8] Itten appealed
to the color theories of Goethe and Runge, as well as
to regularities, harmonious color chords and the color
contrasts of his teacher Adolf Hölzel. His aim was
to create laws about color that were timeless.[9]

Itten's seven color contrasts have proven to be
a helpful introduction to color design:[10]
1. Contrast of hue
2. Light-dark contrast
3. Cold-warm contrast
4. Complementary contrast
5. Simultaneous contrast
6. Contrast of saturation
7. Contrast of extension

Color tones and color harmonies can be generated
with the help of the color wheel - Küpper's in this case.
The use of analogous colors, that is, colors that are next
to one another on the color wheel like yellow, orange and
red, generate fewer differences in color tone and therefore appear to be harmonious, like the color gradation
we see in a sunset.

If you select colors on the color wheel in such a way
that the connecting line has a symmetrical form, like in
the triadic, tetradic and hexadic color chords, harmonious
combinations result. Other options are the combination of
a complementary contrast and an analogous color, or also
asymmetrical color tones as well as bringing in variations
in the saturation and brightness of the color tone.

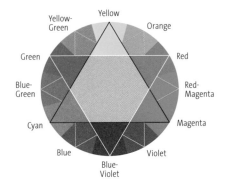

4.08 Küpper's color wheel

3.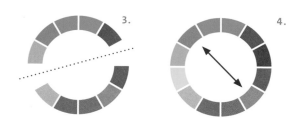

4.

5.

6.

7.

1/4 : 3/4

4.09 Color contrasts acc. to Itten

4.10 Color moods

Colors trigger emotions in us and the effect they have is not constant. Changing color trends and interculturally different color preferences provide space again and again for new impressions and evaluations.

Individual filters
↗ Physiology of perception (eye and brain)
↗ Cultural and social context

Influencing factors
↗ Lighting variations, including geographical conditions
↗ Interaction with adjacent and surrounding colors

4.11 Collages

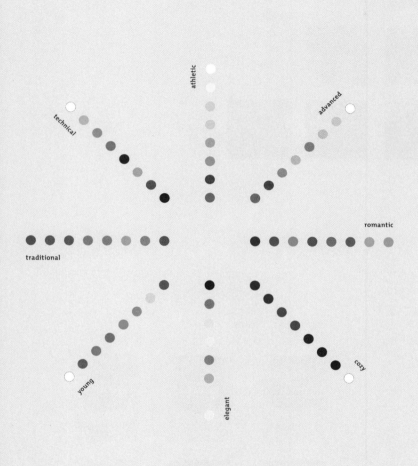

athletic

technical

advanced

traditional

romantic

young

elegant

cozy

4.12 Moodboards

Color collages containing
textures and motifs are used
to establish the basic premises
relevant in terms of color,
form and mood in design, for
example of a corporate identity.

4.13 Abstraction process with a cold-warm contrast

Abstraction process

Color cannot be seen separately from the object. We always have the object that holds the color like a container. It is of no consequence whether the outline is sharp, or diffuse and almost dissolving.

When abstracting motifs, it helps us to analyze the essential components of the object as described in Chapter 2. And when simplifying the color tones, the color wheel, color contrast and the HSB color system are extremely helpful.

Useful strategies are:
Opposites
↗ Highly saturated vs. unsaturated (clouded)
↗ Light (bright) vs. dark (heavy)
↗ Cold vs. warm

Similarities
↗ Analogous colors
↗ Saturation
↗ Brightness and opacity

4.14 The abstraction process when applied in practice

Color preferences are determined by culture and are very different. Nevertheless, we are all touched by a sunrise or sunset, and they both have an energizing effect.[11] And the slow way that the colors change as well as the slow movement of the sun going down have a calming effect on many of us.[12]

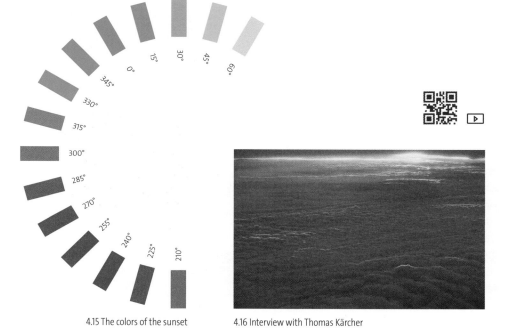

4.15 The colors of the sunset

4.16 Interview with Thomas Kärcher

Color semantics

How we interpret colors has to do with many factors, such as climate, the landscape and the habitat that surrounds us. Among indigenous peoples, for example, colors are often thought of in relation to the surrounding flora and fauna. On the other hand, there are numerous languages that do not distinguish between green and blue. Blue is the color that is least present in indigenous languages.[13] That may sound astonishing, considering we all share the same sky. However, firstly, the sky is not always the same color – it can be pitch-black as well – and, secondly, blue materials tend to be otherwise rather seldom in nature.[14]

In what way and whether concrete color designations can be given in a language therefore depends on the physical environment and, above all, on the importance of the object that bears the color. The established *World Color Survey,* which examined 110 indigenous languages, shows that color designations like black, white and red exist disproportionately often.[15] Black and white, dark and light, are unavoidable indicators of orientation. Red stands for blood, danger and avoidance, and it activates our reaction speed.[16] It is therefore no wonder that nearly all stop signs throughout the world are red.

The ability to recognize colors, however, has nothing to do with our color vocabulary. Indigenous peoples often use comparisons for colors – like the Inuit for example, who live in the Arctic. They have no concrete name in their language for yellow, simply calling it "like urine". All of us – independent of our cultural background – can differentiate between colors, even when they are not explicitly named. Even babies can already tell the difference between the primary colors like

4.17 Santa Claus, 1931

4.18 Catherine the Great, 1787

4.19 *Syndics of the Drapers' Guild,* 1662

red, yellow and blue, and the secondary colors green and purple.[17] The fact that we can even perceive of colors at all has to do with evolution. If we did not have this ability, we humans, and also mammals, would likely not have survived, because if all we could do was tell the difference between light and dark, we would not be able to filter out enough information from what we visually perceive. What is culturally conditioned, however, is how we interpret the colors we perceive of and what associations we link to them.[18]

If we want to be sure that a color is well recognized within the international context, and can also be named and distinguished, then it makes sense to stick to the primary and secondary colors. The colors most easily remembered are the highly stimulating ones like red, orange and yellow. Tertiary colors should definitely not be included when colors are used as an aesthetic medium for communicating information in an intercultural context. The main function of a color is for it to be as recognizable as possible, that is, its recognition factor.

How a color affects us mainly depends on the context. A red traffic light signalizes stop, while red flowers like roses, lotuses or hibiscus are considered inviting in many cultures. Every culture has culturally conditioned and historically embedded color symbols whose meaning and origin are often not clear to us. The color red is dominant in the modern Santa Claus, a figure that plays a role worldwide independent of religion and the meaning he was originally associated with. This has nothing to do with the often-postulated brand color of Coca-Cola but comes from a legendary historical role model from the 4th century AD. This was Bishop Nicholas of Myra, a saint who lived in Lycia, which is located in modern Turkey. Red remains an important liturgical color to the present day for Catholics and the Eastern Church. Nevertheless, the worldwide dissemination of Santa Claus in his red suit may well come from Coca-Cola and Hollywood.

Color also plays a social role. People have always defined their status, the fact that they belong to a certain profession or even their current emotional state to a great extent via the color of their clothing. Before the invention of synthetic and inexpensive dyes, the color of a person's clothes signalized their social status and showed people where they belonged. Expensive colors like crimson, ultramarine and, of course, gold were reserved for the privileged upper class, while everyone else had to make do with monotone colors that were cheap to produce or pale colors like gray and brown. As such, the precious color purple, which was gained with a considerable deal of effort from the magenta snail, was only allowed to be worn in the Antique by the Roman imperial houses and bishops. Interestingly, the norm of associating loud, bright colors with a privileged class changed when it became possible in the 14th century to produce deep black tones. The "noble black" began to move into the world of the bourgeoisie. A change in men's fashion took place throughout Europe after the French Revolution when the aristocracy finally lost its dominant position in society. Following that, men clothed themselves mainly in black, gray, or at any rate in only one color — in all social classes.[19]

Revolutions and liberation struggles have always led to a change in social norms. The following examples from China and Turkey also clearly demonstrate that serious transformation like the separation of state and religion, or the abolition of the feudal states resulted in a change in the colors people wore and their meanings:

In China, following the Chinese Revolution of 1911, there was a break from the colors that were generally used in clothing until then. The abrupt change away from a range of colors, at least among the upper class, to an egalitarian Mao-blue for everyone is no doubt unique to date. For a good half millennium (14th-20th century), the color yellow, a bright golden yellow, was only allowed to be worn by the Emperor and his family and was forbidden for their subjects. The color of a person's clothing served to make their social standing visible to everyone. In the Ming Dynasty (14th-17th century), courtiers were classified according to their rank using the colors red, dark blue and green.[20] This changed with the Chinese Revolution, which equated yellow with decadence and imperialism, instead making bright red the symbolic color of the state, right in line with the Communist color coding.

Another example of a dress code that prevailed for centuries are the color regulations of the Ottoman Empire (14th-20th century). These applied to shoes, clothing, house facades and headwear. In addition to denoting status, the main aim was to be able to distinguish between different religious affiliations. Particular importance was attached to men's headwear. Until the introduction of the fez (a red cap in the shape of a truncated cone) at the beginning of the 19th century, the turban represented status and Muslim religious affiliation for men. For Jewish men, head coverings were pre-scribed first of all in yellow and later in red. And for non-Muslim men like Greek Orthodox and Armenians, the color coding and the head coverings changed over time.[21]

After the dissolution of the Muslim theocracy and the founding of the republic, Kemal Atatürk enacted a law concerning hat-wearing in 1925. It forbade civil servants and public employees from wearing the fez, instead prescribing the European hat that was common at the time. The Dress Reform Law of 1925 also banned women from wearing the headscarf in public institutions. This was overturned in 2013. There was no other country where the type and color of head covering was of such socio-cultural, religious, and perhaps even official state significance, even if head coverings like crowns and feather headdresses have naturally played a role in all cultures.[22]

In summary, one can say that, historically, bright, light and expensive colors initially distinguished the upper class, while dull and lackluster colors were reserved for the lower class. Nowadays, it is more the specific occasion and less a person's status that determines what color they choose to wear. White, for example, is traditionally worn at weddings in the western world, while in many Asian countries white is the color of mourning. The exception proves the rule: religious heads like the Pope wear white every day, while the Patriarchate of Constantinople wears black, and high-ranking Imams and Rabbis wear both black and white.

BUDDHISM	CHRISTIANITY	HINDUISM	ISLAM	JUDAISM

BUDDHISM

✸ Ecstasy, wisdom, insight, submission, incantation, attachment, greed

✸ Life, Tara, strength, exorcism, wisdom, perfection, envy, jealousy

✸ Moderation, nutrition, mirror-like awareness, equanimity, aversion, anger

✸ Delusion, confusion, all-accomplishing wisdom, long life, Tara, peace

✸ Calm, thinking, wisdom, reality

✸ Anger, killing, primordial darkness

CHRISTIANITY

† Love, Christ's suffering, strength, passion, blood, suffering, fire, love, elation

† Trinity, color of the Irish Catholics, hope, paradise, resurrection, life, immortality, the Devil's eyes

† Knowledge, prosperity, bile, envy, betrayal, dishonor

† Maria, heaven, water, truth, faith, loyalty, divinity, spirituality, purity

† God, Jesus Christ, angels, divine light, truth, spirituality, chastity, innocence

† Death, mourning, evil, suffering, sin, pain

HINDUISM

ॐ Source of activity, love, the Sun, Mars, purity, birth, Agni, Lakshami, Shakti, courage, protection, sensuality, the bride, holiness, happiness, marriage, parties

ॐ Festivity, life, joyfulness, peace, coldness, nature, love

ॐ Holy color, happiness, splendor, glory, Agni, Jupiter, Mercury, knowledge, peace, meditation, spring, power of attraction

ॐ Vishnu, Krishna, universality, vastness, love, truth, beauty, nature, heaven, the sea, bravery, protection, manliness, resolve, Prince Rama

ॐ Guna Sattva, knowledge, light, serenity, the Sun, wealth, intelligence, Venus, the Moon, purity, cleanliness, peace, Saraswati, Brahmanen, ceasefire, calm, mourning

ॐ Night, Saturn, anger, darkness, laziness, negligence

ISLAM

☾ Intensity, combativeness, lust, passion, strength, anger, forbidden color

☾ Islam, Mohammed, paradise, complete faith, peace, compassion, holiness, nature, immortality, fertility

☾ happiness, understanding, knowledge, wisdom, perfection, forbidden color

☾ Calm, divinity, spirituality, security, satisfaction, immortality

☾ Holiness, God, unity, virginity, purity, peace, fraternity, harmony

☾ Holiness, suffering, death

JUDAISM

✡ Blood, vigor, origin of man, king/priest, sin, atonement, alarm, wealth, holiness, seduction, earthly desires, impurity, sacrifice

✡ Vigor, fertility, paradise, joy, mercy, natural beauty, reassurance, growth, nature

✡ Transience, illness, old age, leprosy, paleness

✡ Wealth, priests protection, holiness, the sea, heaven, the throne of God, happiness

✡ Full moon, frankincense, health, becoming pure, a lack of sin, joy of life, purity, death, washing the dead

✡ Calamity, bad luck, attractiveness, youthfulness, chastity, orthodoxy, mourning

When synthetic dyes came out of England and onto the market in the 19th century, spreading throughout Europe and soon afterwards worldwide, not only the color palette used in clothing expanded considerably, but also the spectrum of social classes who adorned them. It was European women, for example, who broke with the old conventional socio-cultural color definitions, enthusiastically embracing the new colors – very much in the footsteps of their role model Queen Victoria.[23] Soon, not only the aristocracy began wearing the bright new colors, but also the bourgeoisie and, five years later, saleswomen and working-class women.

Color, which used to strictly define a person's social status, still acts today as an indicator of a person's place in society and also acts to reinforce people's feeling in each case of belonging to a certain group. This can be seen very clearly in political party colors, office colors, occupation-related colors, the colors of team jerseys in sport, or in the colors of religious orders like the brown, white and gray of a monk's robes in the Catholic orders, or the yellow-orange-red-reddish-brown variants worn by Buddhist and Hindu monks, which mark their school and/or religious alignment. It takes rituals, songs, gestures, festivities and customs to live the sense of unity in the respective communities and states, but sometimes the symbolism of colors is enough to express this as well.

What a particular color means to us depends not only on historical, socio-cultural and production-related aspects, geography also plays a major role in this respect. The climate, the seasons, the angle of the sun's rays or the nature of the landscape are all factors that make colors look different and this means they also determine regional color preferences. Colors symbolize something

different in areas with a lot of sunshine than they do in more rainy regions. In the latter, the color yellow is mainly associated with joy, which is less so the case in sunny areas.[24] Strong sunshine, by the way, makes yellow and yellowish tones appear much more color intensive. This intensification tends to be seen more positively in the duller areas of Northern and Central Europe. In hot and sunny Egypt, intense yellow is associated with strong heat, dryness, drought and thirst, and is therefore seen more negatively.[25] It is also interesting that people in warm regions prefer lightbulbs with cool light, while those in warm regions favor lightbulbs with warm light.[26] The classification of colors into cold and warm ones, which is said in many studies to be the most important characteristic by which colors are differentiated, is something we also interestingly see reflected in personality traits. Active and extroverted characters prefer loud colors like red and orange, while introverted types prefer cool and dark colors.[27]

As we can see, many different factors play a role in both color perception and in color preferences. And yet there are some cases where the way colors make us feel are the same all over the world. A large-scale and ongoing online survey, which began in 2017 and included approximately 4,600 test persons, was the starting point for a study that proves there is a clear tendency towards common feelings about color, at least for certain colors. Feelings like love and anger are mainly associated with the color red, and the strongest emotions are triggered by red and black. These global similarities are even stronger when people belong to the same family of languages or are geographically close. The younger the test persons were (15 – 20 years of age), the more they were found to have in common in terms of color, something that perhaps has to do with

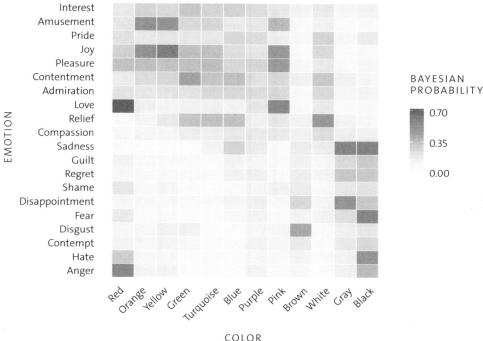

4.21 Results of a study of
universal perceptions of color

COLOR

globalization. There are great differences in the emotions people associate with yellow and purple, whereby you can find many similarities in how people feel about pink, green and turquoise. While red and black, as already mentioned above, were seen to have the biggest similarities in the test persons' emotional reactions to them, the fewest similarities could be found with regard to brown.[28] As only a few or no countries at all in Latin America, Africa, South and East Asia, Australia and Oceania have been included in this research project to date, the results should not be seen as being universally applicable.

All over the world, colors have in the past been and still are attributed specific properties. In western culture, white has been seen to indicate the good and the pure since ancient times, while green stands for hope and red for danger. Such ascriptions, like other traditions, can change over time and can also have different, even contradictory, meanings from culture to culture. In addition to that, when meaning is being assigned to colors, it is important to differentiate between color nuances. In Western Europe, a bright sunny yellow is positively associated with warmth and optimism. Greenish yellow is seen by people there as being fresh, almost cool or even sour like a lemon. Dull yellow is linked negatively to envy and old age because it is associated with sallow skin and yellowed teeth.[29]

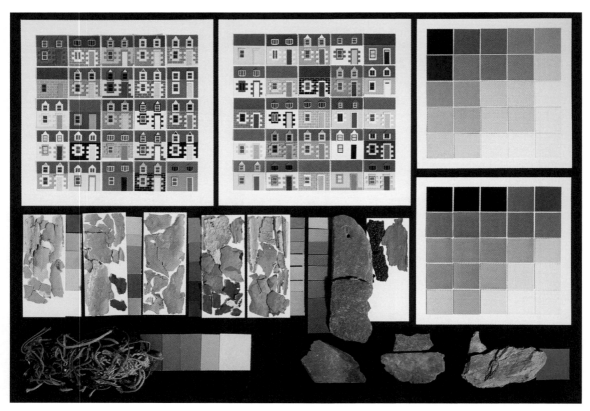

4.22 Methods for analyzing color by Jean-Philippe and Dominique Lenclos

Color Semantics is mainly about examining what thoughts and feelings a designer had when they used a specific color tone and whether their idea ultimately ties in with the thoughts and feelings of the person looking at it. Colors are a very strong means of expression in non-verbal communication. We can make a strong impact when we use them - in traffic signs for example. However, we can also cause ourselves problems by using the "wrong" colors. The color white, for instance, is traditionally associated with funerals and mourning in Japan. Which is why you should never bring your hosts white flowers when you are merely paying them a friendly visit. These historical, cultural and also individual differences in the attribution of meanings to individual colors make the scientific field of Color Semantics as broad as it is complicated, but also highly interesting. The overview table shows numerous meanings of colors from different cultural regions and religions.[30]

But not only psychology and linguistics are interested in the meaning of colors. Color Semantics are just as important in the area of intercultural marketing. Here it is extremely important for the success of a brand whether culturally specific color meanings are taken into consideration in the region where something is being marketed. Regions are compiled into clusters and divided up, for example, into geo-religious cultural areas that are predominantly Christian or Muslim, etc.[31] It can make sense to divide things up in this way, as there are traditional color codes in different cultures or religions. As such, the color gold is often used in interior designs in the Arab cultural region and can be found in highly expensive products, as it is a symbol of luxury. This is not the case in some western contexts, where gold is sometimes associated with being wasteful.[32] The political scientist Samuel P.

Huntington, whose focus was on the "clash of civilizations", also divided up the geo-political cultural areas. The way he did this makes sense if you want to gain a rough overview of the cultural regions, but must not be understood as a rigid classification, especially as globalized civilization is moving more and more away from religious identity. In addition, such classifications often only reflect the predominant way of looking at things based on a specific cultural region.

Another research method that is particularly useful for creative and design professions was developed by the French designer Jean-Philippe Lenclos and his wife Dominique. For more than 50 years, they devoted themselves to a special practical research method in art, which they applied first in France, then throughout Europe and later in Latin America and Australia. They documented, analyzed and classified the way colors were applied and how frequently they were used in rural and urban landscapes. They found studies of building facades and their narrative, synthetic presentation of material samples, watercolor drawings, photographs, and color palettes particularly insightful when researching into color moods. Their goal was to preserve the historically relevant and regional richness of color and, in addition, to avoid non-traditional color schemes in urban planning. Their method, which they called the "geography of colors", influenced architects and designers worldwide in their conceptual and practical design work.[33]

THE WESTERN WORLD
EUROPE, NORTH AMERICA, AUSTRALIA, NEW ZEALAND

- ● Manliness, love, power, energy, Communism, erotic, hot, positive, strength, danger, anger, rebellion, the Devil, prostitution, warning

- ● Nature, ecology, money, happiness, fertility, the environment, manliness, freshness, health, inexperience, envy, jealousy

- ● Joy, happiness, warmth, the sunshine, freshness, jealousy, envy, unfaithfulness, persecution

- ● Manliness, truth, coldness, reliability, cleanliness, calm, professionality, dignity, authority, trust, neutrality, purity

- ○ Purity, truth, spirituality, cleanliness, the bride, joyfulness, elegance, peace, sterility

- ● Exclusivity, power, seriousness, strength, formality, sexuality, fear, mourning, death, evil, sin, emptiness, anger

LATIN AMERICA
ARGENTINA, CHILE, PERU, COLOMBIA, MEXICO, VENEZUELA

- ● Love, passion, joy, power, success, manliness, war, courage, warning

- ● Nature, environment, hope

- ● Joy, the Sun, riches, friendship

- ● Vastness, trust, calm, heaven, freedom, infinity, hope, health

- ○ Purity, coldness, cleanliness, respect, mourning, virginity, placidity

- ● Mourning, fear, death, death, authority, formality

ARAB WORLD
(cf. ISLAM, P. 141)

SUBSAHARAN-AFRICA

- ● Strength, mourning

- ● Fertility

- ● High rank

- ● Heaven, God, often defined via associations without using a word for the color

- ○ Victory, purity

- ● Age, maturity, masculinity

EASTERN EUROPE
RUSSIA, POLAND, CZECH REP., SLOVENIA, HUNGARY, ROMANIA

- ● Love, beauty, passion, Communism, medicine, fear, jealousy, anger, warmth, speed, feelings, Victory Day

- ● Nature, calm, medicine, serenity, reliability, protection

- ● Joy, nature, envy, farewell, the Sun, confusion, activity

- ● Hope, purity, peace, serenity, seriousness, coldness, intellect

- ○ Relief, intelligence, cleanliness, innocence, freshness, wedding, elegance, new beginning

- ● Mourning, fear, death, anger, refinement, silence, emptiness, pacification

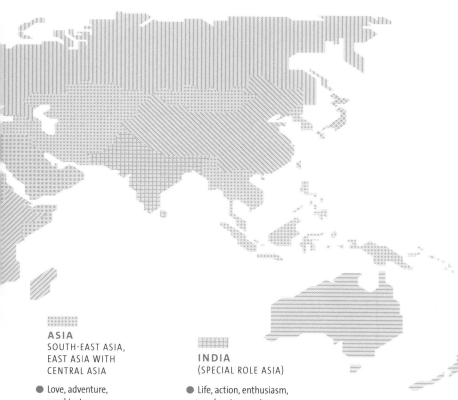

4.23 Cultural areas and the meanings of their colors

JAPAN
(SPECIAL ROLE ASIA)

● Love, energy, speed, strength, passion, the Sun, warmth, attentiveness, joyfulness, anger, danger, blood, sacrificial death, protection

● Love, joyfulness, youth, vitality, nature, endless life, healing

● Good taste, courage, grace, the sunshine, danger, vitality

● Quality, trust, heaven, life, purity, calm, stability, loyalty, coldness, youth

○ Holiness, purity, honesty, goodness, reverence, simplicity, cleanliness, the bride, purity, sterility, trust, innocence

● Power, the unknown, exclusivity, sophistication, formality, sexuality, mystery, depth, regret, non-being, bad luck, fear, evil, mourning, anger

ASIA
SOUTH-EAST ASIA, EAST ASIA WITH CENTRAL ASIA

● Love, adventure, good taste

● Purity, adventure, the spring, youth, birth, desire, danger, illness

● Happiness, good taste, earth, power, royalty, the Sun, manliness, happiness, holiness, neutrality, heroism, mourning, authority

● Quality, heaven, water, trust, coldness, sadness

○ Purity, innocence, morality, the west, the fall, death, mourning, bad luck, nature, neutrality, respect

● Exclusivity, power, water, secret, life, stability, the unknown, wealth, health, death, mourning

INDIA
(SPECIAL ROLE ASIA)

● Life, action, enthusiasm, royal caste, marriage, birth, fertility, humility, sacrifice

● Peace, hope, nature

● Holiness, the Sun, promise of happiness, Vaisya (merchant caste), peasants, commerce

● Love, truth, charity, heaven, the ocean

○ Perfection, Brahman, extreme joyfulness, the holy cow, milk, creation, rebirth, light, serenity, reincarnation, widows

● Untouchable, demonic, infernal, laziness, anger, intolerance

CHINA WITH TAIWAN AND HONG KONG
(SPECIAL ROLE ASIA)

● Happiness, the Sun, love, Chinese New Year, danger, Communism

● Nature, peace, freshness, hope, unfaithfulness

● Harvest, riches, power, earth, the fall, security

● Reason, wisdom, clarity, coldness, mystery

○ Death, mourning, purity, relief, neutrality

● Seriousness, depth, fear, death, stability, the unknown

Ghada Wali, Egypt

Ghada Wali was born in Egypt in 1990. She was one of the first design students to graduate with a BA from the German University in Cairo and followed this degree with an MA in Design from the IED Istituto Europeo di Design in Italy. In 2017 she represented the Middle East and North Africa at TED and was the youngest female speaker at the event. She founded Wali's Studio in Cairo in 2018. She has won several international awards including the Adobe Design Achievement Award and the AIAP Women in Design Award. Wali developed an Arabic font that was chosen as one of the 100 best works of graphic design in the world. Her work has been shown in exhibitions worldwide.

Glitter and glamour prevail on the cover "Chicalastic Music Video". The style and color scheme are reminiscent of the disco scene and hip hop. The jeweled sunglasses are gaudy, attract attention and have "bling".

The Limited Edition soft drink cans are particularly well-staged in these photos, in terms of design. Highly saturated, loud primary and secondary colors are used, both for the background and for the "Woman Sudan" with the red chain, in the can of that name.

4.24 Chicalastic Music Video, 2020

4.25 Pepsi Limited Edition "Woman Sudan", 2020

4.26 "Mirinda Magic" for Egypt and Saudi Arabia, 2020

Hanny Kardinata, Indonesia

Hanny Kardinata was born in 1953 and has significantly influenced the development of Indonesian graphic design over several decades. He established his "Citra Indonesia" design studio in 1980, and also founded the Institute for Indonesian Graphic Design (DGI). He is the author of "Desain Grafis Indonesia dalam Pusaran Desain Grafis Dunia" [Indonesian Graphic Design in the Whirl of World Graphic Design], 2016, the first (and, thus far, only) history of Indonesian graphic design. He has won several international prizes, including ones from Creativity International Awards (USA) and Art Direction Magazine (USA).

The image on the left shows Guruh Soekarnoputra, the eldest son of the President of the Republic of Indonesia, Sukarno. He is depicted wearing a brown tuxedo and a traditional sarong (wraparound skirt), which was not uncommon in the Dutch colonial period (until 1949) and here indicates the balance between tradition and modernity. The colors are predominantly earthy and unsaturated, as in the typical Javanese and royal parang batik of his sarong. The rich red of the sash and parts of the background stand out in the homogeneous color scheme.

"Buatan Indonesia. Mengapa Tidak?", can be translated as, "Made in Indonesia. Why not?". This promotional poster encourages national shopping, as many Indonesians have preferred foreign products over the last century, and in some cases still do. The color red also plays a role here, a major rather than a minor one. The shopping bag contrasts with the background to attract attention. The headline is set in Helvetica Bold with very tight line spacing. The style of this photo collage is international.

4.27 "Guruh Soekarnoputra", 1979

4.28 "Buatan Indonesia Mengapa Tidak", 1987

Shino Suefusa, Japan

Shino Suefusa was born in Japan in 1973 and studied Graphic Design at the Tama Art University in Tokyo. She was awarded a PhD in art from the Tokyo National University of Fine Arts and Music, in 2003. She has been a professor at the School of Design of the Tokyo University of Technology since 2015. Her poster designs have been shown at many international exhibitions and have been selected for collections such as the Danish Museum of Art & Design. She won the 18th Colorado International Invitational Poster Exhibition and was a member of the jury at the International Poster Biennials in Mexico and Bolivia.

The color scheme in the poster "Fukushima Japan" is very subtle and nearly monochromatic. The brownish hue recollects burn marks and refers to the nuclear disaster of 2011. With very small areas for eyes, mouth and nose, an assymmetrical face is shown, almost mask-like, filling the page. The typography is red, and center-aligned, creating balance.

In "The Spirit of Life" series, the brown tones appear washed out and flow like the wet-on-wet technique of Sumi-e in Japanese ink painting. The stenciled motifs are both abstract and concrete at the same time, playing with figure-ground contrast, almost like the Taoist ying-yang symbol.

In the poster "La Nuit dans la Musique du 20e siècle" the little sticks, bent twigs and perhaps pieces of tree bark, seem almost archaic, as in an animistic ritual. Only the pure red, small, rectangular elements stand out.

All of these posters have a paper texture and convey a haptic, sensual experience. By contrast to the digital media world, sustainability and commitment can be felt in these pieces.

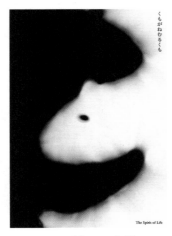

4.29 Poster series: "The Spirit of Life", 2013

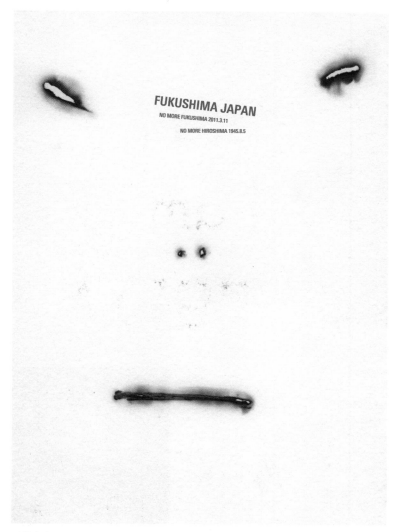

4.30 Fukushima Japan, 2011

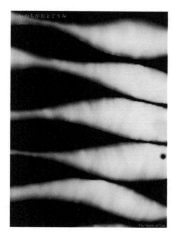

4.31 Poster series: "The Spirit of Life", 2013

4.32 Poster: "La nuit dans la musique du 20e siècle", 2003

Eduardo Barrera Arambarri, Mexico

Eduardo Barrera Arambarri was born in Mexico City in 1974. He studied Graphic Design at the National School for Art, UNAM, in Mexico. He was an Art Director for Leo Burnett, Mexico, and Creative Director for Magic Moments Agency for Communication, Vienna, Austria between 1999-2000. Since 2001, Barrera has worked in his own studio, *neurografisimos,* where he practices corporate design and creates posters for cultural events. His work has been exhibited in many countries and appears in trade publications. He was awarded the bronze medal at the International Biennial of the Poster, in Mexico, and won the Grand Prix at the Biennial in Brünn.

Across cultures, the color red has the strongest signal effect. In Latin America, it implies power, war, masculinity, but also passion and love. The color red dominates all three posters shown here, flanked by black and sometimes white.

In the "Unite for Children" poster, the small white paper boat at the center provides a good example of quantity contrast, as only a small white space is needed to create the focal point. We associate the color white with innocence and the black objects of the background with fear and death.

White also comes to the fore in the headline of the "Comida" poster. The unusual central motif of a heart and the dynamic composition reinforce the dramatic effect. By contrast, in "Dante" the small black figure on the gray staircase is not contrasting, is rather subtle and is staged on a staircase, reminiscent of the optical illusions of M. C. Escher.

4.33 l. to r. Unite for Children, Unite Against Aids, Dante comida

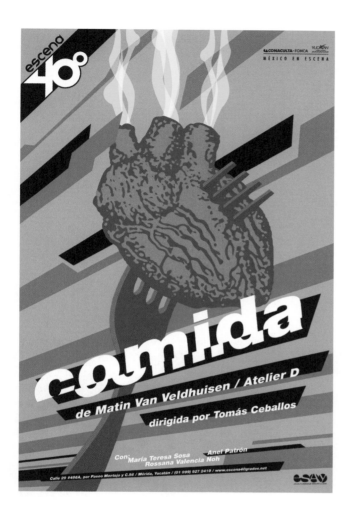

Leo Lin, Taiwan

Leo Lin is a designer, educator and curator. He is a professor and deacon of the College of Arts at the National Taiwan Normal University and was President of the Taiwan Poster Design Association from 2014 to 2016. His work has been recognized with a Taiwan National Design Award, along with other prizes and accolades from leading design organizations and publications across the globe, including D&AD, New York ADC, and New York Type. His posters have been selected for the international poster biennials in Warsaw, Lahti, and Mexico, to name a few.

The colors of the poster at right range from dark blue through light blue, to white, providing a perfect contrast. The bright white face has a signal effect without comprising much area, so here, we can additionally speak of a quantity contrast.

The background color is a cold blue, which symbolizes the sea. The poster has a high level of meaning, accomplished with an economy of means, entirely without type.

4.34 "Global Warming", 2009

Sophia Shih, Taiwan

Sophia Shih earned her MFA in Graphic Design at Boston University and completed a course of special study at Yale University, USA. She has been Professor of Design at the National Taiwan Normal University in Taipei since 2001. Shih is Managing Director of the Taiwan Poster Design Association and the Graphic Design Association of the People's Republic of China, and from 2011 to 2013 was Vice-President of Icograda (now known as ICo-D). Shih combines Chinese and western characteristics in her creative work to represent her philosophy of international design. Her passion for human rights is reflected particularly by her posters.

The balloon-like objects stand out in contrasting, light, unsaturated colors against the dark purple of the background; only the black hand has a similar tonal value to the background. The yellow Star of David, in a highly saturated yellow, and the pale pink necktie push themselves visually into the foreground, due to a strong contrast with the background. The cane and the high-heeled stiletto present similarly unsaturated hues and are the only ovelapping elements. The meaning is explained via the text, set in a sans serif.

4.35 "Fair Election", 2015

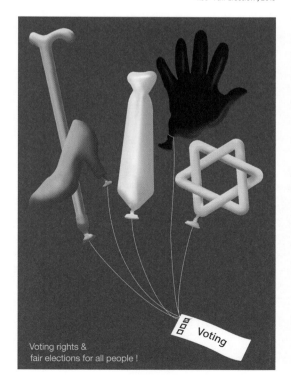

O'Plerou Geret, Ivory Coast

O'Plerou Geret was born in 1997 and is a graphic design student from the Ivory Coast. He took an active interest in art as a child and after a great deal of practice and experimentation with Photoshop, resolved to create an emoji that invoked Africa and post it to Instagram. He gained 2,000 new followers within the first few weeks of the project.

With these emoji, O'Plerou Geret has given social media in Africa an independent, visual identity. In part, these emoji have regional connotations and represent Black people and People of Color. In some specific cases, they are understood only within a cultural context and are not universally comprehensible.

Unsaturated colors are used almost exclusively. The designs oscillate between high and low contrast, with icons contrasting successfully with their backgrounds. Some appear mask-like, others reminiscent of silhouettes.

jeune-homme-masai

wotro

tektek

fanorona

ashanti-stool

cauri

awale

masque-punu

danseuse-dan

femme-himba

femme-kikuyu

femme-mursi

akorou-koffie

homme-wodaabe

homme-touareg

boule-boule

pousse-pousse

cabine

pousse-cafe

4.36 African Emojis, 2018

Lulu Zhao, China

Lulu Zhao is Deacon of the School of Sino-British Digital Media Art of the Luxun Academy of Fine Art and professor at the School of Arts and Media at the University of Salford, UK. She graduated from Qing Hua University and wrote her doctoral thesis on the subject of visual communication design. She works for the National Academy of Fine Arts, in Stuttgart. She was named one of the "20 Greatest Artists in 20 years of Chinese Contemporary Design".

The posters below are from a series developed for the 12th Chinese Sports Games, for a Chinese national audience. They show a monumental staging of bodies in motion, recollecting European futurism and socialist-influenced design. The composition is based on analogous color sequences such as blue-violet, blue, turquoise and red, orange, yellow. The bodies display white and light colors against darker backgrounds. Loud, rich colors and large image motifs dominate the design.

4.37 Poster of the 12th Athletic Games of People's Republic of China, 2013

Ping Mu, China

Ping Mu was born in China in 1994. She lives and works in Shanghai as a media artist and graphic designer. She received her BA from the Shanghai Institute of Visual Art (China) in 2017 and her MA in Experimental Communication from the Royal College of Art (UK) in 2020. Ping's art is largely related to the digital age and cyberspace. Her research focuses on feelings of change and displacement, caused by technology's saturation of our lives.

Here, the Internet is the starting point for a critical reflection: "...the Internet turns people into data," Mu comments. In the computer game "Human Playing" a human being mutates into a robot-like creature of his own uploaded data. Cool colors such as blue, green and a cool pink dominate and become mapped — as if by chance — as gradients and patterns, onto the still incomplete, three-dimensional, wireframe object (a robot-like creature). Location and time-upload data are displayed in a minimalist sans serif.

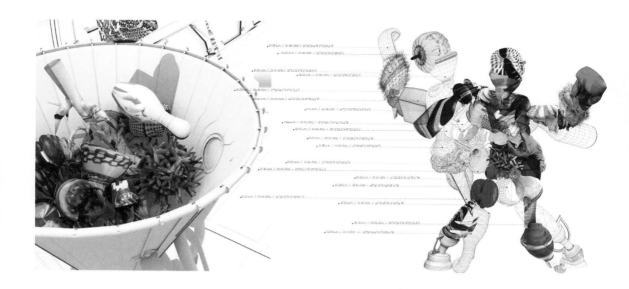

4.38 Human Playing, 2019

4.39 Design: Branding of Haizhu Square in Guangzhou, 2019

Jing Yang, China

Jing Yang is a professor at the College of Design at the South China University of Technology. She supervises students in the area of visual communication design. Her teaching philosophy is deeply rooted in local Chinese culture. Her courses focus on teaching practical skills and stimulating innovation, while taking the very latest trends and design philosophy into account. Jing Yang is a member of the AIGA (American Institute of Graphic Arts).

The branding of the popular Haizhu Square in the city of Guangzhou is based on the combination of a hexagonal mark and an elegant script font. The hexagon, laid out in analogous colors, appears to be a three-dimensional folded object, in contrast with the calligraphic wordmark.

JIng Xiao, China

Jing Xiao is a professor, master tutor and guest scientist at the Guangzhou Academy of Fine Arts of Tsinghua University. She is a national member of the Design Committee of the China Packaging Federation, Deputy General Secretary of the Design Committee of the Guangdong Packaging Association, Director of the Guangzhou Creative Industry Association and founder of the Font Contract Designers.

The design for the graduate exhibition of an art academy is loud, provocative and urban. The appealing character of a cold-warm color contrast dominates. The warm yellow-red tones push themselves into the foreground, while the cold blue tones recede, forming decorative finials to both selected letters and geometric forms.

4.40 Quantum City, 2019

Cross-cultural studies

In the following, national color designations and the color-based traditions lived in three countries — Mexico, France and Indonesia — are presented. The aim of this is to examine different cultural spaces and different geographical locations. Starting at the Greenwich or zero meridian, Mexico is located to the very west on the world map. Despite being located geographically in North America, Mexico represents the Catholic South America. There the Day of the Dead is celebrated, in Spanish the Dia de Muertos, a highly symbolic public holiday that is also celebrated in many other Latin American countries, like Peru and Ecuador for example. France is located in the middle between Mexico and Indonesia, and both the French Revolution and French colonialism have greatly influenced world politics. Its symbol is the French flag, the Tricolore. Indonesia — to the very east — is the largest majority Muslim state that is a pluralistic society and practices freedom of religion to the present day. The state doctrine is expressed in the so-called Pancasila, which has brought forth five guiding principles for the nation.

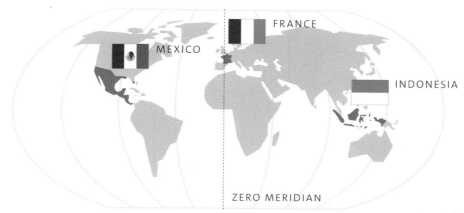

4.41 The Greenwich meridian

Mexico also has a symbol that is just as rich in tradition and as strongly colorful. The Día de Muertos, or the Day of the Dead, is a public holiday that is recognized by UNESCO as an Intangible Cultural Heritage. It originates from pre-Columbus times and is therefore more like a joyous, colorful party than a sad funeral. Color coding plays a significant role in indigenous cultures, something that is known, for example, from the *codices* (pictorial manuscripts) of the Mixtecs.[34] Their dyeing of fabrics was so professional that a blueish dark red produced using cochineal insects suppressed the expensive-to-produce purplish-red in Europe. Fabric dyes from Central America that were produced from plants were a valuable trading good exceeded in value by gold and silver only. The most successful export hit in the 17th and 18th centuries was Indigo blue.[35]

On the Día de Muertos, the prehistoric traditions of the Aztecs and the Mayas and other indigenous peoples merge impressively with the ceremonies of Catholicism that were introduced in the 16th century by the Spanish colonizers. This makes it something very special, and it was recognized as such by its inclusion in UNESCO's list of Intangible Cultural Heritage.

"The Mexican... is familiar with death. (He) jokes about it, caresses it, sleeps with it, celebrates it. It is one of his favorite toys and his most steadfast love." This quote from the Mexican poet Octavio Paz clearly illustrates that life and death are understood as a dialectic union, an endless process that is celebrated equally on the Día de Muertos by both the deceased and the living members of a family. Similar traditions that remember the dead in a joyous manner are found more seldom outside of Latin America. In addition to the black clothing of mourning, the Roma also wear a vibrant red tie or blouse as an additional color. Red stands here for life, as Roma traditionally believe that, until they are buried, the deceased exist in an intermediate state.[36] And in Romanian villages, brightly colored crosses on graves tell unadulterated truths about the lives of the deceased, another example of a colorful expression of mourning.[37]

ALTAR WITH SACRIFICIAL OFFERINGS ON THE DÍA DE MUERTOS

Colorfully decorated and edible skulls made of sugar welcome the dead into the realm of the living.

Photos of the dead: Only those whose photos are commemorated may leave the realm of the dead for a day.

Candles light the way and are at the same time a Christian symbol of remembrance.

Silhouettes made of different colors of tissue paper symbolize the wind and the fragile nature of life.

Something to quench the thirst of the dead after their long journey.

A sea of flowers made from fragrant marigolds show the dead the way to the altar.

The favorite foods of the deceased.

The Pan de Muerto imitates the bones of the dead.

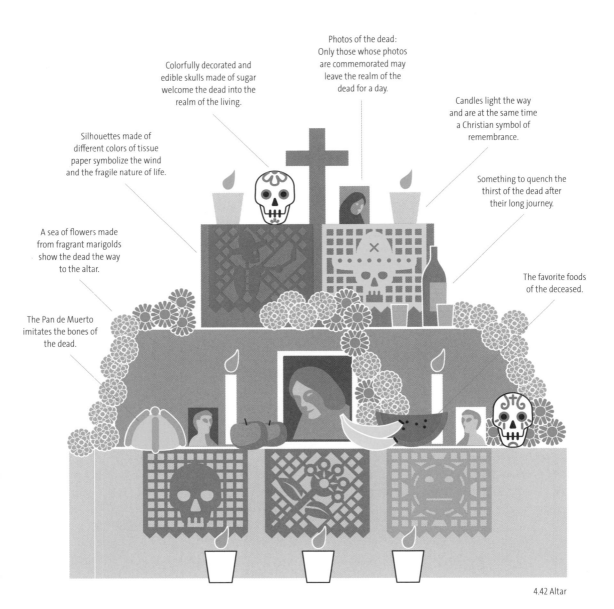

4.42 Altar

From October 31 to November 2, the Día de Muertos honors and commemorates the memory of the dead for three full days. Every day has a different focus. The first day is dedicated to the children who have died without being christened. On the second day, the Catholic holiday of All Saints, all other dead return to their families and are welcomed at the family's home altar with sacrificial offerings. The altar is a central part of the celebrations and is located in the family home or in front of the house, as well as in public spaces like community buildings or schools. There are even competitions awarding the most beautiful altar a prize.

On the evening of November 1, Mexicans go to the cemetery bearing the favorite foods of their deceased family members in order to celebrate together with the dead. The entire graveyard is illuminated by candles and the atmosphere is boisterous and easygoing. People remember the dead lovingly, but also teasingly, toasting them with tequila, and dancing and playing music until the morning. Sweet, wildly colored skulls made of sugar icing or chocolate, colorful silhouette pictures and intensely fragrant, orange-yellow marigolds are a must in every region. Their role is to welcome the dead souls as guests. Sometimes a comb, some soap and a towel are also brought so that the souls of the dead can freshen themselves up after their long journey.[38]

The Día de Muertos is first and foremost a colorful festival and it has a certain similarity to Hallowe'en for outsiders because of the skulls (Calaveras) and skeletons (Calacas). The symbolism of the colors changes and cannot be clearly specified. There are fewer single, monochrome colors dominating the altar and the grave, with multi-colorfulness as the main color concept. Only the bright orange of the marigolds (Tagetes) stands out. Their English name "marigold" refers the Virgin Mary and a Christian

background. Pathways strewn with the Tagetes are there to lead the dead to their sacrificial offerings at the altar. Like the candles, they are there to guide the spirits.[39] The Tagetes were already known to the Aztecs as a healing and ritual plant.[40] The colors yellow and orange stand for life and represent the sunlight.

The colors violet or purple originate from the process of Christianization by the Spanish and represent pain, grief and suffering in the Christian sense. This association is based on Jesus's ordeals on the way to the crucifixion, which is described in the Gospel of Mark as follows: "The soldiers led Jesus away into the palace (that is, the Praetorium) and called together the whole company of soldiers. They put a purple robe on him, then twisted together a crown of thorns and set it on him.[41] The color purple therefore represents All Saints and Lent in Catholic countries, meaning it is also associated with death. A violet flower like the Calaverita, a type of orchid, also known as the "flower of the souls" refers to grief.[42]

4.43 Skulls made of sugar

4.44 Festive parade in typical outfits

4.45 French national holiday, Louvre, Paris

The French flag, the Tricolore, has three colors and originates from the time of the French Revolution. It consists of blue and red, the colors of the city of Paris, and the royal white of the Bourbons. All three colors are based on France's history which, from the early Middle Ages onwards, was closely linked to Catholicism. As such, the French medieval kings carried the Oriflamme into battle as a sign that they were the "true" defenders of Christianity. The red Oriflamme was the holy banner of the Abbey of Saint-Denis de Paris and referred to the blood of the martyr Saint Denis, the city's first Archbishop who remains the patron saint of the French to the present day. That is where the color red in the French flag comes from.

During the uprisings at the beginning of the 1789 Revolution, the blue and red cockade established itself. It was a symbol pinned onto caps that identified the prerevolutionary city militia. Later on, the Jacobins — a political society — also wore it on their red caps. The red liberty caps of the Jacobins were the symbol of opponents of the monarchy. Red therefore became the color of revolution, and the raised fist has been an international symbol of resistance since the beginning of the 20th century.

The color blue stands for royalty, which can be seen in the popular, but rather loosely defined term "royal blue". The proper term is "ultramarine", which was originally made by grinding the valuable lapis lazuli stone. It was used in medieval Europe to refer to the power and significance of religion and the monarchy. The blue cloak of the Virgin Mary, Jesus' mother, and also the coronation robes of kings are evidence of this. It is also what the blue in Paris's coat of arms refers to.

The color white came later and, in 1794, it became the emblem of France six months after the monarchy had been toppled. The white fleur-de-lis banner of the Bourbons was regarded as the incarnation of the traditional monarchy before the French Revolution. Why was the color white then chosen when it represented the monarchy? This was mainly because the bourgeoisie were not hostile to the monarchy and wanted to have a constitutional monarchy. It was probably the moderate General Lafayette, the General of the National Guard, who had the idea of adding the monarchic white to the colors of the city of Paris, blue and red.[43]

By contrast, the white fleur-de-lis banner remained a hostile symbol of the Bourbon monarchy and Paris's state prison the Bastille, and therefore a symbol of repression for the workers and the petit bourgeoisie. The storming of the Bastille was the flashpoint of the French Revolution.

Only 10 of the world's 196 flags contain the colors red, white and blue in a vertical or horizontal arrangement. The colors red and blue form a strong warm-cold contrast, but with similar brightness so that the contrast can hardly be seen in poor lighting. The white in the middle helps ease this and provides for clarity and visual order. The interplay between all three colors has a strong impact and works very well from a distance.

4.46 Church coronation of a French monarch

Indonesia, the country of many peoples, proclaimed its independence from the Dutch colonial power in 1945, whereby this was not officially signed until three years later. Indonesia was run by a foreign power for a total of 350 years. Before that there was no Indonesian nation, but individual kingdoms that were first of all Buddhist, then Hindu and, from the 15th century onwards, mainly Muslim. Only Bali continues to have a majority Hindu population today.

Parallel to that, there are many indigenous peoples who practice their own religions. There are many different ethnic groups who have their own languages, like the Malays, the Minangkabau people (a matrilinear society), Polynesian peoples as well as a Chinese minority. The country is also not geographically uniform, as the population is spread over more than 6,000 of the altogether 17,000 islands.

It is therefore easy to understand why the political motto "Unity in Diversity" intended more than anything else to achieve the country's independence as a nation together.

The motto is not new and originates from the Majapahit Empire (13th to 16th century), the most powerful and last Hindu kingdom with its main seat of power in Java. A philosophical theory, the so-called "Pancasila", aimed to ensure a new identity-forming solidarity and was already declared by Sukarno, Indonesia's first president, in 1945. This guiding principle, which is based on five individual principles, is so broadly termed and kept so general that it is acceptable to all political and religious groups.

To date, there is no single official interpretation. Each individual is left to interpret it as they see fit, something that is typical for Indonesian society in which the individual has the right of interpretation, and society's value system is marked by harmony and consensus. Sukarno emphasized that it was not he alone who created the Pancasila, saying that all he did was bring together the wishes and aims of the Indonesian people that had developed over time. His successor Suharto also had no doubts concerning the *Pancasila* but made use of its strong symbolic power. *Pancasila* is therefore more of a national ethos and lived praxis than a state doctrine.[44]

4.47 Tropical flora

4.48 Tattoo and state emblem *Gardua Pancasila*

The *Pancasila* was to be symbolized later in the form of a recognizable state emblem. Sultan Hamid II was commissioned with its design. The symbol is called the *"Garuda Pancasila"* and was officially introduced in 1950. The emblem has remained unchanged to the present day and is based on Hindu-Javanese mysticism. The golden bird, the Garuda, is throned at its center. It plays the role of a divine messenger in Indian mythology and symbolizes both strength and power. It holds a ribbon with the motto "Unity in Diversity" in its claws and wears a shield containing the five guiding principles of the Pancasila on a chain around its neck.[45] Nothing is left to chance, and every form is highly symbolic. The 17 feathers of every wing, the right feathers of the tail and the 45 feathers on the neck refer to the day of independence August 17, 1945.

The five principles are presented on the shield in the form of easily understandable symbols.

1. In the middle there is a gold star on a black coat of arms: Belief in the One and Only God.
2. A golden chain on a red background: A just and civilized humanity.
3. A green Banyan tree: Unity of Indonesia.
4. A black bull's head on a red background: Democracy led by inner wisdom in consultation/representation.
5. A golden rice sprig next to five buds of cotton: Social justice for the entire people of Indonesia.[46]

4.49 Yellow rice cone served at festive meals, called Tumpeng

The first principle clearly presents the model of a nation state that includes the existence of religion in the state. That is a special feature in today's world, when one bears in mind that 87% of Indonesians are Muslim and only 11% Christian. Hindus, Buddhists and Animists make up the rest. All other principles of the *Pancasila* are just as complex and cannot be further explained at this point.[47]

All colors of the state emblem also have a meaning of course. The color gold/golden yellow decorates the Garuda and stands for dignity, majesty, magnificence, glory, honor and prosperity. In Javanese healing ceremonies (Indonesian: Slametan), for example at the birth of a child, yellow rice is often served as part of the sacrificial offerings. It is a symbol of hope in salvation through God. At weddings, traditional and valuable gold accessories like tiaras, earrings and necklaces as well as gowns embroidered elaborately with gold are customary. In this way, the bride and groom embody the god and goddess. The meaning of gold/golden yellow is described in a comparatively reduced fashion in the law of the Republic of Indonesia. This states that the color yellow symbolizes "the greatness of the nation or the magnanimity of the state".[48]

The color green is associated with the hope of living a fulfilled life in harmony with nature, which provides us with everything we need.[49] Green also symbolizes wealth, which might have to do with the fact that, in the past, the agrarian sector of the economy played an important role and, even today, a third of the population are farmers.[50] In the traditional, courtly context green is worn at weddings, for example, and at coronations. Green therefore stands for the aristocracy and thus also for nobleness and magnanimity, which is associated in Javanese culture with the hope of a better life. Javanese believed that the king had to provide for his people and enable their growth. This idea still applies today and has been transferred to the people's representatives who are supposed to provide for the citizens.[51] Little can be found in corresponding legislative decree about the color green. Perhaps this is so because green is one of the essential colors of Islam and people wanted to avoid any controversy.

The color red has played a role in the mythology, literature and history of Indonesia for a long time. It generally cannot be mentioned without also mentioning its counterpart white. Red and white are the colors of the Indonesian flag, which is based on the banner of the Majapahit Empire (13th to 16th century). Many Indonesians today still long for this pre-colonial age to return. Majapahit is repeatedly cited as a role model today, for example in connection with South-East Asia as a historically famous maritime hub, something many would like to see again today.[52]

The banner of the Majapahit Empire is called the "palm sugar flag" (Indonesian: gula kelapa). Palm sugar is reddish in color and remains an important ingredient in Indonesian cuisine. What exactly the association with palm sugar means remains unclear, but the following interpretation makes sense: The palm is an important raw material for building houses, for coconut milk, for charcoal made from the shells and for palm wine. It was a multifunctional, essential and very abundant component in people's basic supplies. Red might also stand for economic supplies and, what is more, the color red can be associated with the sweet palm sugar, making it very easy for people to internalize.

4.50 Flag of the Majapahit Empire

4.51 Indonesian flag

Another interpretation takes a linguistic approach and is based on Austronesian mythology, as Indonesian or Malayan are founded in the same family of languages that are spoken to the present day in Malaysia, on the Philippines, on Madagascar and in parts of Thailand, Vietnam, Cambodia and China.[53] Here, the colors red and white symbolize Mother Earth and Father Sky. A dual concept that is actually known from the creation mythologies of Indonesia.[54] In Hindu philosophy, the colors red and white stand for the two elements of conception, namely Kama Bang (the woman's ovum, the menstrual blood) and Kama Petak (the man's sperm).[55]

Bearing this in mind, it becomes easier to understand the following quote from Sukarno: "The colors (red and white) were not just decided for the Revolution. The colors came from the beginning of human creation. The blood of a woman is red. Sperm is a white man. The sun is red. The moon is white."[56]

In addition to this, red symbolizes courage, the fighting spirit and bravery, a meaning that has only existed since independence. Since then, the color white has been given a clear meaning for the Indonesian population: *"Red is the symbol of bravery, white is the symbol of purity."* The link between purity and the color white can also be found in the Jasmine petal, which is Indonesia's national flower. It is also associated with purity, honesty and modesty. And on Java, the Jasmine flower is also the flower of weddings. The color white has mainly positive connotations in Indonesia.

The color black represents the circle of life and people's connection from the beginning of creation to the end of all life.[57] Black symbolizes permanence and eternity.[58] In Javanese society, the spiritual meaning of black is truth, wisdom and equality. The traditional clothing of most Javanese men was also black, which stands for courage. An unbending will, historically with masculine connotations, is one of the historical cultural values of the people of East Java.[59]

The *Garuda Pancasila* symbol is also seen by most young people in a positive light. The popular folk song *Garuda di Dadaku* (*Garuda* in my heart), of which there are many different versions, and which is sung at football matches, for example, demonstrates the positive national unity.[60]

4.52 Animations based on Augmented Reality

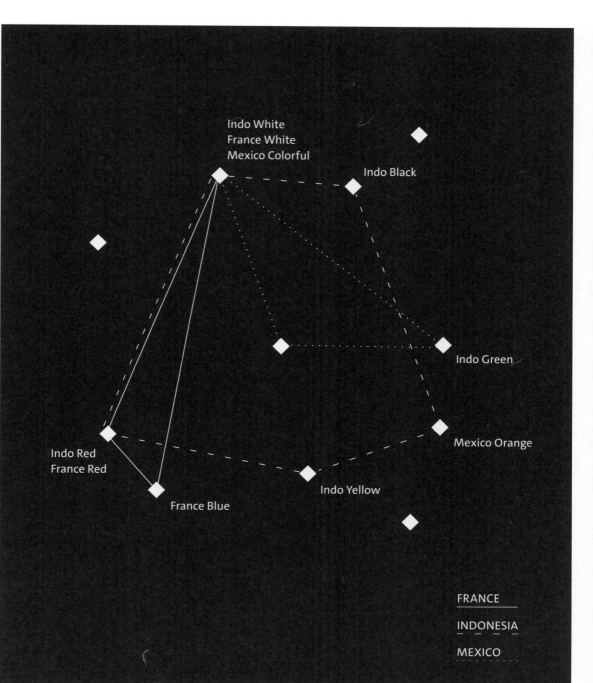

Indo White
France White
Mexico Colorful

Indo Black

Indo Green

Mexico Orange

Indo Red
France Red

France Blue

Indo Yellow

FRANCE

INDONESIA

MEXICO

Colors: Egypt, Ethiopia, India

Katrin Hinz has been giving workshops on
Color Theory and Universal Design Thinking at different universities since 1995. They
often start with the following 10-minute
warm-up exercise: within a maximum of
10 minutes, students are supposed to
compose a color tone that they find very
pleasant and attractive using a minimum of
2 and a maximum of 5 colors. After that, the
results of the color exercises are presented
by having the students hold them in front
of their bellies. Interestingly, at least one of
the colors chosen is nearly always the same
color as the respective student's eyes, hair
or a piece of their clothing.

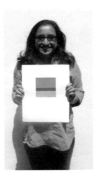

4.53 Students in Bangalore at the National Institute
of Design India with their "likable" color combinations, 2014

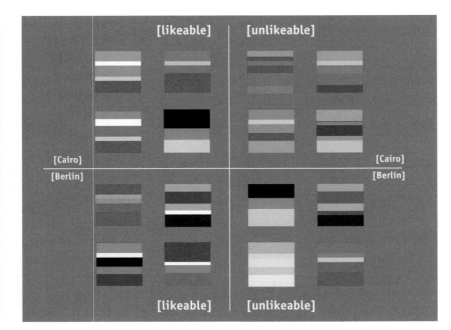

4.54 Color codes:
German University Cairo

4.55 Museum Wukro,
Ethiopia: target group types
for the museum's educational
work with traditional hairstyle
and modern clothes

In the second exercise, an unpleasant and unattractive-looking color tone is to be produced. This has proved to be difficult to date because, despite all their efforts, the design students often end up creating a harmonious and pleasant color tone. They tend to find unpleasant colors in the work of the others.

This shows that color is judged in an extremely subjective manner. It also clearly shows that, despite globalization and the fact that our "consumer tastes" are becoming more similar, clear differences can still be identified among the different countries.

When the exercise described above was carried out in Cairo, the favored color tones that resulted used fresh, light and cool colors like green, turquoise and blue in combination with yellow or white, as well as black, red and gold as color tones with positive associations. Dark and very warm color composi-

tions were considered pleasant. The experiment took place at the German University Cairo, the logo of which bears the German national colors black, red and yellow, and this had an influence on the favored colors. A positive association with the German national colors is astounding and likely demonstrates more the students' identification with the elite university than with Germany. The cool colors green, turquoise and blue come from Islamic tradition, where these colors are sacred and you can find them everywhere in architecture, art and artisanry.

In India and Ethiopia, strong colors dominate in everyday life and religious contexts, and this is reflected in the color combinations. This was the subject of a 2015 workshop for an archaeology museum in Wukro, Ethiopia. The project partners preferred culturally embedded and highly saturated colors for the museum's educational materials for Ethiopian schoolchildren.

4.56 Pictograms for the Wukro Museum
in Tigray, Ethiopia, with adaption of the national dress, 2015

Please describe your educational background, including your studies, work/study, and travel.

I grew up in the GDR and live in the former East Berlin. I traveled extensively in Eastern European countries as an adolescent. My interest in culture, history and architecture comes from my family. My father was an architect, while my mother worked in Berlin's state museums. They encouraged our interest in culture early on. I began studying Architecture at Weissensee Art Academy when I was 20 and, after gaining my degree, worked as an architect and a stage designer. Then, right after the Wall came down, I opened an office with my sister, a designer.

In 1994, I started working as the founding professor of the new study course in Communications Design at Berlin's HTW university. From 2002 to 2004, I began my involvement in the Faculty of Applied Science and Art at the German University in Cairo. This was followed by study and research trips to India, Ethiopia and China. I have been Dean at HTW, Berlin in the faculty for Design and Culture and, since 2019, Founding Dean at the Design Faculty of GIU AS.

What countries or cultures have you worked with closely and/or lived in? Have you had formative experiences in other cultures?

Most of my teaching experience was gained in Egypt and India. I learned very intensely what everyday work as a designer in another culture was like in Ethiopia. The most intense experiences I have had were in everyday life in Egypt, so I would rank them: 1. Egypt, 2. Ethiopia and 3. India.

What did you know about these countries/cultures before you started working together?

I was theoretically well-prepared, but it was like jumping in at the deep end. When I worked in Cairo for half a year in 2008, and was confronted by a new culture, I could fall back on my earlier experiences from Eastern Europe. Growing up in the East also helped me, because being able to improvise and always have a plan B up your sleeve were skills you needed in the GDR. There were many parallels between the GDR and the Mubarak system.

Katrin Hinz
Studied Architecture at the Art Academy Kunsthochschule Berlin Weissensee, German Democratic Republic.
Currently professor at Hochschule für Technik und Wirtschaft Berlin, University of Applied Sciences / Founding Dean at *German International University of Applied Sciences* (GIU AS)

4.57 Workshop in India with participants and Katrin Hinz
4.58 Students in Bangalore at NID India with their likable color combinations, 2014

What specific differences have you noticed in how students learn in other countries/cultures?

German students often experience an epiphany when they come into contact with other cultures and realize that western culture is not superior. I experience how strongly their religious background influences the way that international students think and act. Islamic students question things less at the beginning and tend to want more rules. Their visual perception is more two-dimensional, which is a result of the Muslim ban on images. Their understanding of spatially abstract presentations is less marked. However, all of my students have a great curiosity and open-mindedness, and cope with steep learning curves impressively – no matter where I have taught and worked.

Teaching or working in a culture different from your own involves adapting to different social and moral norms, including issues of class and gender. What has your experience been like in these areas, and in what ways did you adapt your working or teaching methods as a result?

The fact that I am a female has never been relevant. I have always been respected in my professional and management role. Perhaps it has to do with my age and my height. I'm five feet eleven. Although I conform with cultural rules and norms in the respective countries, I do still touch upon uncomfortable political and religious topics, like my interest in Jewish culture, or social inequality. Self-censorship is not my thing, and I already forbade myself from practising it in the GDR. My teaching methods are aligned towards international design education. I develop my teaching contents from the respective culture of the countries I work in.

What are the benefits you have gained from working in countries/cultures that are different from your own culture?

You never stop learning. My work in Cairo, for example, has made me more conscious of my own cultural and aesthetical origins. Our European aesthetics are greatly influenced by the Orient. From 2014–15, I carried out a design project for a new museum with German students in Ethiopia. We developed and implemented the corporate design right up to the exhibition design in cooperation with the Ethiopian partners. While struggling to come up with a logo, the Ethiopian side said they wanted it to express "dignity".

We were surprised and the students realized that "dignity" had never occurred to them as an attribute. Empathizing with another culture is a key to intercultural communication and, in Wukro, the new Archeology Museum is the absolute pride of the community and represents the dignity of their thousands of years of history.

5.01 International design workshops in Indonesia, Germany, Uganda and France

INTERCULTURAL EXPERTISE

Working together in international teams is an established practice in the media and IT industries. It is very interesting, but it can also present challenges. These are caused by different cultural influences that we are generally not even aware of. They are reflected in our daily behavior, our verbal and non-verbal communication and above all in our value systems: "A job well done" is highly respected in all the industrialized nations. However, the way that people strive for and achieve their goals is evaluated very differently. While in the nations of northern Europe and North America are considered to be "task-oriented", the nations of East Europe, Latin America, Africa and Asia tend to be more "relationship-based."[1] Understanding, accepting and making use of such different value systems is vital when international teams work together.

I visited a German friend in Yogyakarta several years ago. She has lived in the Indonesian city on Java for many years. Shortly before I was to return home, I wanted to buy a present, preferably off the beaten track away from typical tourist locations. We went into a shop and I immediately started choosing souvenirs. Unlike me, my friend chatted with the shop owner about his store, his family and his grandchildren. I finished my shopping quickly, stood around doing nothing and waited for her. I felt like we were wasting time talking to a stranger. My friend didn't know him ei-

ther. When we left the shop, she told me off and I learned my first lesson in relationship-oriented communication.

In many countries in Asia and in the Arab countries, encounters that concentrate purely on an impersonal transaction are unusual, or even impolite. There are other cultural differences in the areas of communication, trust, scheduling and deciding, to mention but a few.[2]

That is why I prepare my students for their encounters and cooperation with other international students, familiarize them with general rules of conduct, clothing norms, etc. and allow them to get to know one another before a workshop starts. Despite, there are always surprises and flexibility is required.

Intercultural competence in the media

In my intercultural workshops, I have been researching since 2009 into how the participants in international teams work together, what needs and demands they have, and how their learning situation can be optimized. My teaching approach is based on the one hand on a praxis-oriented progressive pedagogy that supports "learning by doing"[3] and, on the other hand, on critical-constructive didactics that allows students to gain competence.[4] This is added to by the fact that learning and experiencing in an intercultural context and abroad are much more demanding and requires greater communication skills than are generally needed within one's own cultural environment. Therefore, additional pedagogical strategies and practical methods are needed to deal with the lack of knowledge about the other culture and the differentness.[5]

When working together with design students of mixed nationality, intercultural competence should be achieved so that cultural, social and individual barriers can be removed. The participants learn international working methods and design styles, which improves their intercultural media competence, flexibility, tolerance, respect and communication skills, which in turn motivates them to expand their horizons. The goal of the intercultural workshops is to create skills that enable the students to operate internationally and to apply what they have learned every day when they are home again.

The four cornerstones for successful competence are:
↗ Problem-solving competence – in order to overcome difficulties
↗ Social competence – in order to work in teams
↗ Professional competence – in order to work with factual knowledge
↗ Self-competence – in order to act self-reflectively, self-confidently
   and responsibly

Intercultural competence consists of a bundle of different skills. It begins with observing ourselves and, from there, discovering differences and common features between cultures. You first have to understand and reflect on your own position and culture before you can enter into a meaningful dialog with someone from another culture. One analogy is that you must first know your own language well before you can successfully learn a new language. Intercultural understanding therefore plays a decisive role. It means grasping other cultures, living circumstances and contexts so that you can interpret them properly and respect them. It also means being able to change your own perspective in order to make that happen. Only then can an intercultural dialog take place – with a focus on willingness to cooperate and an awareness for your own cultural system of orientation.

In my intercultural workshops, internationally mixed groups of participants meet at a place or at least in a virtual space, where they work in a specified timeframe of 3 to 5 days on a task that is relevant for all participants from their different nations and allows for an intercultural comparison.[6]

In this setting, the participants get to know one another, talk to one another and question their own value systems. One Indonesian participant said in an interview, briefly and succinctly: "We had to meet each other in the middle".[7] That isn't so easy and requires us to be able to put ourselves emotionally in the shoes of others and to successfully change our perspective.

The following are vital when acquiring intercultural competence:
↗ Self-reflection and self-knowledge
↗ Mindfulness and attentiveness,
↗ Open-mindedness, tolerance and flexibility
↗ Estimation and acceptance of other cultures
↗ Self-confidence

To achieve intercultural competence, animation - and especially Type in Motion - is one of my preferred media. Animation is movement. Every movement has meaning. To move something, people also have to move themselves and in doing so also move their current position and way of thinking. When a team of students wants to create an animation, they have to agree on a topic and a storyboard, to animate and transform shared objects like types and images, as well as synchronize music. Animations are a helpful pedagogical tool that bring the students together and allow them to tell a story together.[8]

INTERCULTURAL COMPETENCE

5.02 Characteristics of intercultural competence

Stereotypes

The chosen workshop topic should ideally contain the important cultural characteristics and specific national features of all of the students involved. The key question when trying to find a topic is – what makes us different and what connects us?

We all have culturally and individually determined outlooks, stereotypical presumptions and judgements when it comes to other cultures. That is a valuable starting point for an intercultural coming together. Presuppositions do not necessarily have to be negative. They are like boxes we use to navigate our way through our complex environment and they help us react fast to new and unknown situations. But stereotypes also have disadvantages. They do not take into consideration a person's individual characteristics or uniqueness.[9] They do not take into account the specifics of a situation. They can have a negative impact if they are not continually examined and corrected. There is a risk that they will become generalized prejudices and might even turn into xenophobia, racism, homophobia or sexism. Unlike stereotypes, which are not necessarily negative, prejudices are based on ill-considered emotions and often on opinions adopted from others without thinking. They are always negative.[10]

For my 2011 workshop at San Francisco State University, I chose "Stereotypes" as my theme, as the students taking part had different genders, as well as different geographical, ethnic and religious backgrounds.

In the preparation phase of the workshop, the students explored in different ways their mutual ideas about being German and American. One team used Google search terms like "Germans are…" to find and collect stereotypes about Germans or Americans, which they then used in a humorous way afterwards to perform video interviews. This gave the students a more easygoing introduction to a complex and controversial topic.

In the workshop proper, the student teams decided on sub-topics like eating habits, family, ecology or patriotism. In the conceptual phase, the topic became more focused using brainstorming and mind-mapping, and then worked out thematically in storyboards and realized in an animation.

Stereotypical ideas of other cultures can be best reduced via direct contact, differentiated education and stays abroad for that purpose. It is also very advantageous to do this by working as part of a project and above all by having a shared goal.[11] It can ultimately be said that both the American and the German students realized that their assumed stereotypes were often wrong. What is more, friendships formed between both nationalities that went beyond the workshop.

5.03 Animation: "The Oracle", San Francisco, 2011

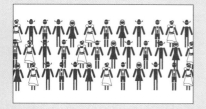

5.04 Animation: "Family", San Francisco, 2011

Please describe your educational background, including your studies, work/study, and travel.

My first Design studies began (2 weeks after Woodstock) in September 1969. This was at St. Lawrence College in Kingston, Ontario, Canada. After this three-year course, I worked for a year and a half at "Jet Signs", a sign shop run by two Germans, Horst and Rosemarie Wolf. In the mid-70s I moved to Ottawa and worked in print shops, litho studios, even silk-screening hockey sweaters at a sporting goods store. I eventually had a position referred to as "programmer" at Campbell Computerized Typesetting Systems. Various jobs followed and in the mid-80s I decided to return to education.

I finished my Bachelor's in Visual Communications in 1987 at the Nova Scotia College of Art and Design, Canada. Then I ran a design office with my partner Elizabeth Owen and taught at NSCAD before moving to Germany in 1992. There I worked on type design projects at MetaDesign in Berlin.

I was a founding member of the new faculty at the Bauhaus-Universität in 1996. In 2016 I officially retired, but I continue to teach there.

What countries or cultures have you worked and/or lived in/with extensively or closely? Have you had formative experiences in other cultures?

I had teaching gigs over the decades, but primarily in "Western" situations, until I was invited in 2006 to teach at the National Institute of Design (NID) in Ahmedabad, India. I was invited back several times (I guess they were satisfied with my teaching) and ran a project on wayfinding and signage systems. I've also taught at several design schools in China – in Wuhan, Guangzhou and Hangzhou and I maintain contacts there.

What did you know about these countries/cultures before you started working together?

Not much more than the clichés. But my prejudices were quickly dispelled upon working with the students.

What specific differences have you noticed in how students learn in other countries/cultures?

Our school in Weimar uses a rather open method of teaching, expecting independence and originality from the students. My experiences in India and China generally tended to show more rote-learning kinds of situations, but with exceptions. My experiences in Ahmedabad and Bangalore in India were most rewarding. Students and staff there came from varied backgrounds throughout India and were open, flexible and creative.

Teaching or working in a culture different from your own involves adapting to different social and moral norms, including issues of class and gender.
What has your experience been like in these areas, and in what ways did you adapt your working or teaching methods as a result?

The tendency in Design education in Europe is moving toward more and more female students as time goes by. I find this a welcome development and I hope there will be a more balanced culture within the design community in future. This applies all over the world, and of course not only in design. Universities generally tend to attract students from higher-earning family backgrounds. There are of course exceptions, but teachers have to remember that this demographic doesn't represent society as a whole.

What are the benefits you have gained from working in countries/cultures that are different from your own culture?

I was given a wake-up call with regards to my own assumptions regarding what Design students in general might know. I taught an "Introduction to Typography" course for Master's students in Information Design at the PG (Post-Graduate) campus of the National Institute of Design at Gandhinagar, Gujarat province, India. I assumed that Master's students would have a similar educational background to those from western cultures and had a lecture prepared on the subject of "Form Follows Function". My plan was to expose the true origins of this expression – an article from the late 19th century by the American Art Nouveau architect Louis Sullivan – but was surprised to learn that the students had never heard this expression. It took the wind out of my sails, so to speak, and I had to change the lecture on the fly, explaining what most people assume when they hear this expression. It was like ruining a joke by having to explain the punch line. My take-away was a reminder of the old adage: "never assume – it makes an ass out of you and me. (ASS/U/ME)".

Jay Rutherford
Studied in Kingston, Ontario and Halifax, Nova Scotia, Canada, but learned by training on the job
1996–2016 as a professor of Visual Communications at the Bauhaus-Universität Weimar, Germany
Currently collaborations with design colleagues and public art projects

"What is normal?"

Only very few students are familiar with the land and culture of their host country. They are first of all confronted with new and, above all, unknown impressions. These can be strange smells, unfamiliar foods or different noise levels. My "What is normal?" workshop began with an extensive exploration of the city of Yogyakarta in Indonesia, which was also documented. The photos, sketches and sound recordings were analyzed on the following day and discussed with the Indonesian participants. They were really surprised that the German students were so unsettled, for example, by the level of street noise and the public transport, which was normal for the Indonesian students. Examining your own perceptions and working them into your design work is part of all creative work and can be exercised particularly well in a strange environment.

The Indonesian students supported the German students by offering them possible interpretations and practical tips, such as not waiting for the bus to stop at the bus stop, but to give a clear hand signal that you want it to stop. Signs are understood on the basis of agreement and are an important foundation for communication. If you do not speak the local language, then you can communicate with the help of gestures, for example, when you need to name a number when buying something. However, counting on your fingers is not known in every culture. This was used by one team as the basis for their animation.

In the conceptual phase of design work, it was important to not only visualize the perspective of the German students to the urban signs and symbols in Yogyakarta, but also to equally bring in the perspective of the Indonesian students. Only when that happens is an intercultural examination of signs possible.

5.05 Workshop, Yogyakarta, Indonesia, 2014

5.06 Animation: "culture shock", Yogyakarta, Indonesia, 2016

5.07 Animation: "Using hands as a sign", Yogyakarta, Indonesia, 2016

Please describe your educational background, including your studies, work/study, and travel.

I studied Interface Design at Potsdam's University of Applied Sciences from 2003 to 2007. In my third year, I moved to Graz, Austria to study there for a few months.

Since graduating in 2007, I have worked as a user interface designer, app developer, and typography expert. I teach regularly at design schools in Austria, Denmark, Germany, and Switzerland. I travel to speak at design conferences throughout Europe a few times a year.

What countries or cultures have you worked and/or lived in/with with extensively or closely? Have you had formative experiences in other cultures?

In 1998, when I was still a teenager, I spent a semester in Wichita, Kansas, in the United States, staying with a host family and attending public high school. I had gone on language study trips to the US before that when I was even younger. This exposure at an early age to environments where nobody spoke my native language was certainly an experience that helped me reflect on cultural perspectives later in life.

My other intense intercultural experiences began in 2010, when I started teaching two-week app design courses every year at Copenhagen Institute of Interaction Design (CIID). Lecturing as part of this international Master's program means spending every day with a class of students with diverse ethnicities and cultural backgrounds. In a class of 25 students, there are often 15 or more different nationalities.

What did you know about these countries/cultures before you started working together?

I have always been interested in languages and—being a typographer—I have a detail-obsessed interest in text and writing systems. My favorite way to learn about other countries and cultures is to speak with as many people as possible from these countries. And, of course, balancing these personal experiences with factual knowledge that is readily available on the Internet is helpful to complete the picture.

Most of the international students I know who spend only one year in Denmark can't be bothered to learn Danish. After a few years of teaching my two-week courses in Copenhagen, I did start to learn Danish at evening school in Berlin. Not because it's useful (it's not), but because I became interested in how the pronunciation maps to the written language.

What specific differences have you noticed in how students learn in other countries/cultures?

The international students I teach in Copenhagen have very diverse cultural and professional backgrounds. The school's one-year Master's program features many courses that are experimental, speculative, or even artistic. It has a very strong human-centered approach that makes it easy to bring up and discuss cultural differences among the students and staff.

What I have seen, especially in more recent years, is that the students have a lot in common in how they learn the things that they are most interested in: by watching YouTube tutorials! In that sense, the globalization of learning has already happened.

Teaching or working in a culture different from your own involves adapting to different social and moral norms, including issues of class and gender.
What has your experience been like in these areas, and in what ways did you adapt your working or teaching methods as a result?

One difference I noticed was the varying degrees of formality and respect that students show for the teacher's role. In my experience, European and American university students tend to see their teachers at eye level, while Asian cultures in particular show more respect or even avoid openly disagreeing with the teacher's perspective.

Frank Rausch
Studied Interface Design at the University of Applied Science in Potsdam
Gained teaching expertise in Sweden, Austria and Switzerland
Since 2009 Managing Partner at Raureif in Berlin

What are the benefits you have gained from working in countries/cultures that are different from your own culture?

Interacting with a highly diverse mix of students from different parts of the world lets me reflect on my own behavior, cultural habits, and expectations.

My favorite example is how the design feedback you give depends strongly on your own cultural background. Together with my teaching partner and long-time business partner Timm Kekeritz, I even made a chart to (half-jokingly) illustrate this: When someone from Germany calls something "interesting", they probably mean it's great, while someone from California may say "interesting" to express that they find it absolutely terrible. Making the students aware of this at the beginning of the course is useful; every time someone says "interesting" in the following days, someone else will usually ask: "Which kind of 'interesting' do you mean?"

5.08 International comparison of feedback in design

Understanding Design Feedback

INTERNATIONAL

Bad   Okay   Good

CALIFORNIAN

Interesting   Awesome

GERMAN

Scheiße   Interesting

BRITISH

Interesting   Interesting

Bilingual and trilingual proverbs

All cultures have a wealth of national and regional proverbs and sayings. These are an excellent source with which to get to know cultural and geographical idiosyncrasies, and many of them include farm animals and house pets, for example. This is demonstrated in the Javanese proverb "Cedhak kebo, gupak", which literally means "if you are close to the buffalo, you will be exposed to the mud". Water buffalo are typical farm animals in Asia, while they are more seldom in Europe, North and Latin America and in Africa.

Indonesian, Greek and German students took part in my 2017 workshop. The aim was to design typographic animations that look at proverbs and to emphasize words that are important for the content of the proverb, such as water buffalo. Proverbs with a similar message but with different details were to be presented, like the English proverb "If you lie down with a dog, you will get up with fleas". In addition, three different type systems were applied: historical Javanese, Greek and Latin.

Beauty ideals were also examined, as in the 2010 workshop, with the well-known Arab proverb: جه يكحلها عماها which means: "He wanted to beautify her by applying kohl to her eyes, but he blinded her instead", which means he meant well, but caused damage. Eyeliner originally comes from the Near East, North Africa and South Asia and is used all over the world today.

Proverbs are like icebergs: the visible part is what we think we understand, but the majority of their historical and cultural meaning is unknown to us. That is exactly what makes them valuable for a closer examination of another culture as well as our own culture.[12] They are "cultural metaphors" and act like "language-based image constructions, are cognitively intuitive and socially effective".[13]

5.09 Workshop, Ulm, Germany, 2017

5.10 Animation of the proverb "If you lie with a dog, you will get up with fleas" i Latin and historical Javanese script, 2017

5.11 Arab proverb: "Mention a cat and it jumps in", Cairo, Egypt, 2009

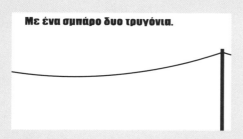

5.12 Animation of the proverb "Kill two birds with one stone" in Greek, Latin and historical Javanese script, 2017

Please describe your educational background, including your studies, work/study, and travel.

I was born and grew up in Namibia and moved to Berlin to study Graphic Design. My design class was the last to be educated without computers. Retrospectively I realise that this provided us with a good foundation in design thinking. At the time, without the internet, designers and visual artists were not easily accessible for exchange and inspiration. It was my typography teacher who sparked my passion and respect for typography, and in the late 90s I designed the font Dropink for Linotype.

Throughout my career I attended workshops, conferences and training to keep up to date with new trends and ideas. In my current position as art director I manage the corporate design of the Charité, a public service institution. I regularly supervise trainees/interns, and discovered my passion for teaching. I have worked with Bayimba, a cultural institution in Uganda, their academy hosts various workshops and regularly invites me to teach.

What countries or cultures have you worked and/or lived in/with extensively or closely? Have you had formative experiences in other cultures?

I am influenced by the German-Namibian culture. At that time, Namibia was under the occupational rule of South Africa and as a result of the apartheid system, the society was segregated along racial lines. I wanted to get out of this society, and moved to Berlin. During my studies I was engaged as a graphic designer in the Anti-Apartheid Movement.

I spent most of my professional life working for the Charité and freelancing for projects in Namibia, South Africa, Angola, India, Tanzania, Kenya and Uganda. After the first democratic elec-

tions in South Africa I lived in Durban for two years, freelancing for an agency specialised in educational and social-political projects.

What did you know about these countries/cultures before you started working together?

Having lived in Africa, I immediately felt at home in Uganda. I love being there, and am very interested in my students' ideas, hopes and dreams. It's an exchange, I teach skills and in return I learn about my students' distinctive urban culture, the Ugandan social situation, creativity and professional possibilities. I am inspired to share my knowledge with young designers in Uganda and hopefully in more countries in the future.

What specific differences have you noticed in how students learn in other countries/cultures?

The biggest difference is that students in Uganda have an appreciation for the training and value knowledge. Access to the internet is expensive, few students have access to online tutorials. Students are keen to receive feedback on their work and we have very interesting debates about Western visual communication, which often can't be applied, compared to those in Uganda.

Teaching or working in a culture different from your own involves adapting to different social and moral norms, including issues of class and gender. What has your experience been like in these areas, and in what ways did you adapt your working or teaching methods as a result?

The first workshops had only male students but recently it has become more gender balanced, thanks to Bayimbas initiative. My teaching methodology involves presenting design skills and reinforcing the skills through exercises. These exercises are structured in a way to encourage students to develop their own ideas, and to present and portray concepts that will be useful in their professional lives. Groupwork is an effective teaching tool and I noticed that more experienced participants naturally partner up with less experienced students, as communal learning is valued in Ugandan society.

What are the rewards and benefits you have gained from teaching in countries/cultures that are different from your own culture?

I have come to understand that the realities creative professionals in Uganda face in order to complete a project are vastly different to design professionals in Europe. This has increased my respect for their achievements. I also really enjoy the interactions while teaching, which are always in a friendly and humorous atmosphere. Discussions about style, design, communication and aesthetics reinforce my consciousness of how creative and diverse cultures across the globe are.

Christine Voigts
Studied Graphic Design at Lette Verein in Berlin
Since 2003 art director at Charité - Universitätsmedizin Berlin (Medical University in Berlin)
Visiting lecturer at Bayimba Academy in Kampala, Uganda

Collective identity–street art

This intercultural workshop brought together students from Germany and Greece to the University of West Attica in Athens. The topic was, on the one hand, the outstanding street art in the Exarchia district of the city and, on the other hand, the complex theme of collective identity. For the workshop duration, international student teams each formed a group with its own individual character and at best a feeling of being a collective "we". Forming temporary group identities in changing workspaces has become an important part of the global employment market. We are no longer restricted to a conventional work context and, in the area of design in particular, we must further develop our social skills all the time.

At the beginning of the workshop, the students were asked what interests and what outlooks they have in common. In this initial phase, they filled out questionnaires on their outlooks and their design preferences – from minimalistic to playful to ultra-trendy – and then shared these with their team members. Questions like "Who are we as a group?" and "How do we express our group identity in design and stylistically?" were asked at the beginning of the brainstorming.

This was the basis on which one of the following roles was played out:
↗ Intercultural start-up design agency
↗ Urban district initiative/environmental protection group
↗ Fantasy group in gaming or fiction
↗ Another group identity of their own free choice

When the research phase started, there was a photo session in Exarchia, Athens' trendy subculture district. This was followed by lectures on international street art and the mural art scene, and about how graffiti, e.g. illegal tagging, is margimalized. In order to find a starting point from where the students could find their own style direction, a wide range of different styles were analyzed. The outcome of these workshops was deliberately left open so that the students were not restricted in their creativity.

5.13 Workshop, Athens, Greece, 2018

5.14 Animation: Presentation by the Start-Up agency in Exarchia, Athens, Greece, 2018

5.15 Animation: "Philia", Athens, Greece, 2018

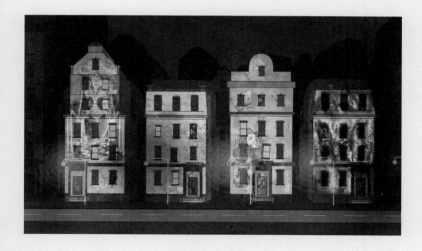

5.16 Animation: "Soul", Athens, Greece, 2018

Please describe your educational background, including your studies, work/study, and travel.

I graduated from Cornell University with a BA in American Literature. My first job was as a one-man art department for a small printing company in Boston where I acquired a solid foundation in all aspects of print production. I was a Principal in a boutique design firm in New York and a Partner in an advertising and public relations agency in Santa Fe, New Mexico. I was co-founder and creative director of a national magazine focused on contemporary Native American art. Now retired, I continue to teach marketing, digital animation, and English language in the US and internationally. I hold a visiting faculty position at a bilingual vocational college in Mexico. I have visited many countries on several continents, and I continue to travel extensively.

What countries or cultures have you worked and/or lived in/with extensively or closely? Have you had formative experiences in other cultures?

My most extensive contact with a culture different from my own was working with Pueblo and Navajo tribes in New Mexico, where I developed tourism and arts marketing programs and published a national magazine. For the past few years, I have worked periodically in Mexico, where I am part of an educational team developing a pilot bilingual vocational college.

What did you know about these countries/cultures before you started working together?

Before working with indigenous tribes, I knew very little about their culture. Over time, I grew to understand the significant cultural differences between Native Americans and non-Native Americans in America, both historically and in the present day. I do not speak Spanish, so my work in Mexico is conducted in English. Working in a country where I do not speak the language presents challenges in understanding cultural differences because I am essentially an outsider whose value is in bringing English language and American values to help create an international culture which is perceived as necessary for the future success of Mexican students.

What specific differences have you noticed in how students learn in other countries/cultures?

Indigenous peoples value or group identity, while non-Indian Americans prioritize individuality and competition. In working with indigenous peoples, the challenge was to balance cooperation with personal achievement. Mexico retains strong colonial and class/racial hierarchies, so the challenge there is promoting equality within the global community.

Teaching or working in a culture different from your own involves adapting to different social and moral norms, including issues of class and gender. What has your experience been like in these areas, and in what ways did you adapt your working or teaching methods as a result?

The main challenge in working with Native Americans was acknowledging their historical distrust of white Americans based on centuries of oppression and accepting my inherent complicity: an apology was necessary in order to move forward in every professional situation. Learning to allow them to tell their stories in their own way was essential in becoming a bridge between cultures. In Mexico, I am always aware that all educational and professional interactions are conducted in a language that is not their own. In valuing their ability to express themselves in English, I communicate in a simpler form of English without condescension while reinforcing their confidence. Since my role involves bringing American values and style to Mexico, I am careful to avoid imperialist attitudes.

What are the benefits you have gained from working in countries/ cultures that are different from your own culture?

An anecdote that best illustrates the benefit I gained from working with indigenous peoples was learning their style of shaking hands. Americans prize a firm handshake, which would seem aggressive to indigenous peoples. When Native Americans shake hands, there is contact without pressure, which can seem weak to Americans. So, in learning to shake hands with Native Americans without applying pressure, I indicated an understanding of their culture which allowed for mutual trust and constructive working relationships. By not imposing my culture on theirs, I was able, in some small way, to overcome longstanding conflict and embody a collaborative attitude which benefited me as well as my colleagues. As a result, my marketing projects and my magazine were successful because they were accepted by Native Americans as genuine expressions of their cultural values, presented in styles that were familiar to them because we all live in America, albeit in different worlds.

Lewis Nightingale
Former creative director in New York and Santa Fe, New Mexico
co-founder and creative director of an artist magazine, focusing on contemporary Native American art in U.S.
Since 2018 design professor at Universidad Tecnológica Metropolitana de San Luis Potosí, Mexico

Praxis-based workshop

Logos, pictograms and icons are of great importance nowadays because of globalization. When used in branding, logos and other style attributes of the brand are either locally anchored or function worldwide. Regional companies that want to advertise and sell their products and services on a global market require a redesign, at best without losing their original identity.

This idea was the basis for the "Signs go global" workshop. The workshop involved a project partner from the real business world. A local brewers, which had its headquarters in Bavaria, declared itself willing to take on this role. This gave the US student group from SanFrancisco State University the chance to learn something about German culture. One team had the task of developing a limited special edition of a beer for the international market. Another team researched into the international history of beer and gave an informative presentation using infographics. The third team concentrated on a comparison of beer adverts from all over the world and made a film collage using the results of their research. In the ensuing presentation, the students were given positive direct feedback from the client. This reinforced their self-confidence.

In the following year, a workshop involving real practical exprience took place together with The Romberg Tiburon Center, the maritime research and teaching campus at San Francisco State University in the Bay Area. The aim of this workshop was to support the center's PR activities for the target group 'families and children'. Animation was to be the medium used, to be shown either as a 30-second public service announcement (PSA) or as an animation series on Twitter.

5.17 Studio Hinrichs, San Francisco, 2013

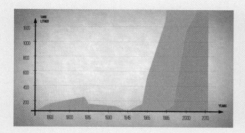
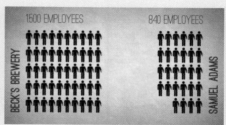

5.18 Topic: A local, German brewery operates globally. Animation: Research into beer as an international product, 2012

5.19 Topic: A local, German brewery operates globally: Animation: Branding campaign, 2012

5.20 Title: Untitled, 2019 / Warped Universe, 2019

Please describe your educational background, including your studies, work/study, and travel.

Born and raised in China, I grew up in a city of 6.4 million. The high competition meant a lot of pressure at school, with classes from 7:30 am to 10 pm. My mum taught art, which I also liked, but it was seen as a risky career option. My dad was a self-made businessman who invested in my education instead of buying luxury goods. He funded my studies at the Royal Melbourne Institute of Technology at 16. I knew no-one in Melbourne but was young and didn't care for risks. A bachelor's in Communication Design started my design career, and an internship in a Melbourne agency saw me working mainly for corporate clients.

I became interested in the culture of Turkish friends in Melbourne, which took me to Istanbul. I had no job or plans at the time but took the risk anyway. Luckily, I found an agency doing web and branding, and learned some basic Turkish. I went freelance after 2 years, but then came a military coup in 2016, impacting the economy and making many people I knew depressed. I mostly worked remotely, so I chose to leave the city for Thailand as a digital nomad.

I loved my freedom there, but a 2017 job offer brought me to the Berlin office of an international agency. Germany? Why not! I flew to Berlin knowing nobody and with no expectations. Things went well, and I set up my own design studio in year two. I switched between agencies, being an in-house designer and independent, as I enjoy both freedom and collaboration in bigger teams. I also like giving talks and sharing my design ideas.

What countries or cultures have you worked and/or lived in/with extensively or closely? Have you had formative experiences in other cultures?

All these cultures influenced me. I would say:
- in Melbourne, the fashions, architecture and lifestyle were alien to me at first. The friendliness there, even to strangers, surprised me. I was once invited to a neighbor's party although I never met her but was too shy to go.
- in Istanbul, the Turkish people were extremely welcoming, and it was so easy as a foreigner to meet new people. But they

Lu Yu
Studied at Royal Melbourne Institute of Technology, Australia
Specialized in web design, branding and art direction, and has experience in agencies as an inhouse designer and freelancer

hugged and kissed a lot, which was very different to China.

- in Berlin, it wasn't easy at the beginning to make friends. The friendship culture there is different again. But, while it took more time, it was very rewarding, and I still keep in touch with people I met from day 1.

What did you know about these countries/cultures before you started working together?

Not a lot. As a young person I just go with the flow, try different things and am not afraid to make mistakes.

What specific differences have you noticed in how students learn in other countries/cultures?

My education in China was rigid, with a strong science focus and a lot of memorizing.

In Melbourne, my degree focused on creativity and tasks were more open for interpretation. It was challenging at first, because I wasn't sure if what was doing things 'right'. I had to learn there are many approaches to a problem.

5.21 Chinese typography: Design makes everything possible, 2016

Teaching or working in a culture different from your own involves adapting to different social and moral norms, including issues of class and gender. What has your experience been like in these areas, and in what ways did you adapt your working or teaching methods as a result?

When I first worked with clients, I was shy as I was taught to be respectful and not challenge my superiors. In Europe I learned to speak up my opinion, earning more respect because of it.

In Turkey, where many think it is a privilege to be a housewife, I felt the gender difference. My career ambitions shocked some people.

In Europe I have more professional opportunities, as startups want diverse teams and only judge people by the work they deliver.

What are the benefits you have gained from working in countries/cultures that are different from your own culture?

There are more opportunities abroad, experiencing other cultures, different food and different people. It opened my eyes, making me an open-minded professional designer, less judgmental of unfamiliar things. But it was not all good. The role of women can vary so much and is vital for me in a culture, both privately and professionally.

While design trends change constantly and the gap between China and Europe is shrinking, the subtle differences in aesthetics are still interesting.

For example, many Chinese people like lots of color and content, feeling it gives them a lot of entertainment value. In Europe, most people prefer minimalistic design, Compare the cyberpunk-like street signs in Hong Kong and Berlin's wide streets with little advertising!

And Chinese characters look more complex than Latin letters, and font limitations in the digital world often mean designs with a lack of visual hierarchy. Which makes some designs look visually busy.

5.22 Card series: Positive word, 015

Social media—cultural differences

Social norms, stereotypes and trends have always existed, but the invention of the mass media has dramatically changed our perception of reality. The media, in its varied forms, is an instrument of social and political influence by special interest groups, individuals and countries. With the help of media technology, people can be influenced in greater dimensions. Photos and videos are increasingly gaining dominance over the written word. And the most important aspect is that simulation can construct a new reality showing something that is not real. Imagine a beautiful sunset with your loved one. What would you do to make it more real? You would perhaps make the colors even better and post and post this singular moment on Instagram. However, this changed picture would no longer be "authentic and real".

To analyze how cultural differences and things people have in common affect people's perception of YouTube commercials, this workshop at the Indonesia Institute of The Arts Yogyakarta used two different approaches:

↗ The usual way applied by designers, which is content-based and draws on impressions, emotions and experiences and falls back on statistical questionnaires
↗ Recording the eye-tracking data while observing a YouTube video with the aim of analyzing the behavior and attention span of the viewers.

The YouTube videos were chosen from the following categories: vlogs, influencers, animations, cooking and baking, as well as advertising for the younger generation, both in Indonesia and in Germany. The main aim here was to create a special setting for the Indonesian and German students that promoted intercultural understanding thus and initiated a dialog between them. This was achieved by trying out different approaches and methods when comparing YouTube videos as the basis for creative analyses. The focus was not placed on the design results, but rather on the process and on documenting the knowledge gained during the exercise.

5.23 Workshop: "Social media–cultural differences", Yogyakarta, Indonesia, 2020

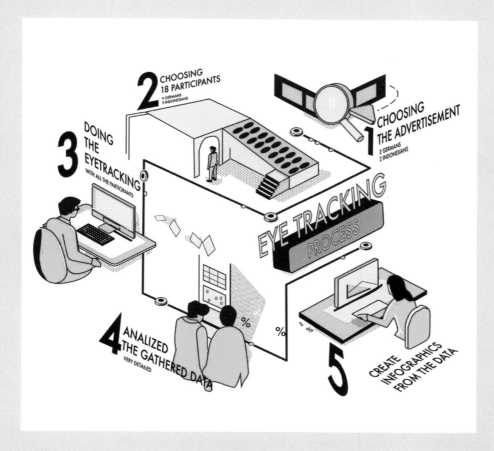

5.24 Research about Indonesian and German YouTube videos using eye-tracking, 2020

5.25 Graphic on the visualization of a German-Indonesian video comparison based on an eye-tracking analysis,2020

5.26 Evaluation for an analysis of YouTube videos, 2020

5.27 Typographic poster in Arabic using the heliotype process in Leipzig's "Lichtdruckwerkstatt", 2012 (section)

Describe your education, your career path so far and your international experiences.

I began my education in my birth town of Mosul in Iraq by doing my advanced-level school qualifications ('Abitur' in Germany) which, following my father's wishes, had a technical focus, especially the skills of a fine mechanic and lathe operator. This knowledge has helped me to the present day, because it requires millimeter precision and I can use that in many areas of my work. Subject matters or practical tasks and their proportionalities become measurable and tangible. That makes things a lot clearer and you can treat the functionality of a micro-area with respect.

I ultimately made my way to Germany to study subjects I was very keen on: firstly Cultural Pedagogy, then Visual Communication.

In what countries or cultural environments have you lived and/ or worked in? Have you had any experiences in other cultural contexts that had an impact on you?

I very deliberately decided to study in Germany so that I could gather new experience here that went beyond my own cultural background. I found that to be a very enriching experience, one that still affects my life today.

After Germany I had a brief period in Romania where I studied for one semester. Because of my position as founding dean of the German University in Cairo, I had an extended period of stay there and I still go there several times a year work. I'm involved in other activities in Qatar, Jordan and in my home country Iraq.

What did you know about these countries or cultural environments before you worked there?

Not more than anyone else knows from the general knowledge they gain in the media. But that's exactly what made me curious. It was like a different research trip every time for me. I like to compare the mentalities and working styles, how people deal with time and resources. There are surprises on every trip, and I can learn from these. You automatically make comparisons and reflect on your own actions than would otherwise be the case. That way you can learn a lot.

Rayan Abdullah
Professor for Typography at the Academy of Fine Arts in Leipzig
2002 Managing director of Markenbau, agency for corporate identity and corporate design, Leipzig
2006 Founding Dean at the Germany University in Cairo
2016 Foundation of Academy for transcultural exchange, Academy of Fine Arts in Leipzig

What specific differences have you observed in the way people learn when you consider students in different cultural environments?

As a university lecturer, I mainly experience students from the German and Arab cultural environments. In all of them, I have noticed that, while they were very curious and open-minded, they are nevertheless strongly affected by their upbringing. They are very friendly and easygoing, but sometimes not very ambitious about their future. They do not shy away from talking about it and are also willing to rethink things if they think that's the right thing to do. Their environment doesn't always make things easy for them. However, they achieve good results that can help them get far in their career.

Working and/or teaching in another cultural environment means adapting to different social and ethnic norms, including possible differences in class or gender. What have you experienced in this area and how has it influenced your working style and/or teaching methods?

Education today not only refers purely to the communication of factual knowledge, but is much more about appropriating methodical skills, that is, the ability to solve problems methodically and independently. It has become more important than ever to communicate the approach towards problem-solving as a process, the valuable experiences that are learned in this process and also the results in a clearly understandable manner.

Access to information crosses borders and cultures and is available all over the globe, but only reflecting about your own cultural identity as a teacher and also as a designer enables you to teach knowledge in a way that is culturally specific, tailored to your learners and authentic. In this way, communicative USP is created with a high degree of professional benefit for both the teacher and the learner in equal measure.

What are the benefits you have gained from working in countries/cultures that are different from your own culture?

I remember one of the first times I was invited for breakfast after arriving in Germany. The host offered me blue cheese and, as I was totally unfamiliar with it, I thought it was highly poisonous. However, when I tasted it, I actually liked the new taste of it, and I gradually began trying out new things, learning new tastes and gathering new culinary experiences. I think that has a lot to do with the childish curiosity I still have and that always leads to me to learn new things. Curiosity remains my loyal companion.

5.28 Letter ornament, exhibit from the exhibition on the art of Arabic script in Berlin, 1993

5.29 Two Arabic points as a detail from a typographic poster in Arabic created using the heliotype process in Leipzig's "Lichtdruckwerksatt", 2012

5.30 Calligraphic presentation of the word "freedom" in Arabic, 2010

Bauhaus and Beyond

This four-day intercultural workshop took place in cooperation with the Indonesia Institute of the Arts Yogyakarta, Indonesia. The workshop was followed by an excursion to the Bauhaus in Dessau and to design agencies in Berlin.

At the beginning, lectures and discussions took place, mainly to familiarize the Indonesian students with the topic "Bauhaus and Beyond". All of the design students had certainly heard of Bauhaus, but less was known about what it meant for each individual student and their development to become a professional designer, or for design teaching.. The term 'Bauhaus' is generally associated with a minimalistic style, without knowing the historical and social backgrounds.

A collection of quotations by teachers from Bauhaus and the "Hochschule für Gestaltung" (HfG, or University of Design) provided a point of entry for exploring guidelines and doctrines like "less is more", and "form follows function". Research into topics like the history of Bauhaus and individual products like the famous Bauhaus cradle, which is made of the shapes triangle, square and circle, was also part of the workshop. A visit to the former Hochschule für Gestaltung in Ulm (HfG, 1953-1968), one of Bauhaus's follow-up schools as well as an exhibition of design products made the special architecture an especially tangible experience.

The aims of the workshop were to expand the knowledge, above all especially among the Indonesian students, of the myth surrounding Bauhaus and to ask questions about a style that is understood as the Bauhaus style. Ornamental designs, like those influenced by Javanese culture, were deliberately integrated and used create a visual contrast.

5.31 HfG Archive in Ulm, Germany, 2015

Conclusion

The concept of my intercultural design workshops has proved its worth in the area of university teaching. The students gain valuable experience for their later professional life and learn about new concepts, methods and design variants in a praxis-oriented, international learning situation. They profit both professionally and personally, become more culturally flexible and break down their prejudices. An additional benefit is that they improve their study-related English skills. These are good prerequisites for an international career. However, their experiences are also useful for them in their home environment when dealing with clients, colleagues and superiors.

In the questionnaires at the end of the workshops, 94% said they would take part again if students from other countries/cultures also took part. The participants confirmed that a 3- to 5-day intercultural design workshop did more to improve their technical and design skills than a considerably longer theoretical course.

This is only a small part of my quantitative evaluation with 97 test subjects from a total of 228 participants from from eleven workshops. In connection with my qualitative evaluation, those questioned often said similar things, and their message was loud and clear:
What contributes to the success of intercultural workshops are at least two different cultures, a workspace, a setting, a topic that is interesting for everyone and a shared goal. If all of these things are in place, almost every media form and many other topics can bring the same results.

All intercultural design workshops:
www.intercultural-design-workshop.de

WHAT WAS MOST IMPORTANT FOR YOU?

↗ **78%** Team members from different cultures
↗ **20%** Topic
↗ **2%** Animation

WOULD YOU PARTICIPATE AGAIN IN AN INTERCULTURAL DESIGN WORKSHOP

if the participants come from other countries / cultures?

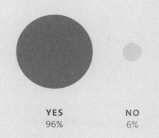

YES
96%

NO
6%

5.32 Evaluation by 97 test persons from 11 intercultural workshops

Please describe your educational background, including your studies, work/study, and travel.

I first chose to be a communication designer for print media. Later I received a PhD in Art/Design/Media from the Bauhaus University, Germany. Currently I am working as an established graduate secondary-school teacher of Fine Arts in research projects.

I first chose to be a communication designer for print media. Later I received a PhD in Art and Design from the Bauhaus University, Germany. I am currently working as an educational councilor in secondary school at higher civil service rank teaching Fine Arts in research projects.

What countries or cultures have you worked and/or lived in/with extensively or closely? Have you had formative experiences in other cultures?

London:
I lived in London for two years directly after I finished studying Design in Hannover. I had many jobs there including as a cocktail waitress, a bartender, a life model, and a waitress in Soho nightclubs. These jobs were certainly formative in many ways.

Cairo:
I lived in Cairo for six years as a single mother with three children. There I held the position of design professor at the German University in Cairo and I was the head of the drawing department for six years.

While at GUC, I created bookbinding and letterpress departments and a clay/gypsum studio. Teaching Egyptian students was a pleasure because they are so kind and polite and most of them work really hard. Today my former students bring the idea of sustainable design and the creation of useful industrial products, as well as bilingual design solutions, into life and into action.

What did you know about these countries/cultures before you started working together?

London:
As a child, I traveled with my parents in the north of England and I liked the atmosphere. My parents had teacher friends in Nottingham who I lived with during my summer vacation in order to learn English.

Cairo:
I grew up in a very open-minded family. My mother, who came from a Swabian village, liked a different way of life. We had guests from many backgrounds, but her focus was on Arab culture. This is surely the source of my own interest in the Arab world.

What specific differences have you noticed in how students learn in other countries/cultures?

While working toward my PhD, I compared the Egyptian educational system with the German system. I found that most of the curricula in Egyptian schools were very similar to British, French, and American ones. It is as if they had no confidence in their own culture and language. I think this is a vestige of colonial times. Especially in design, acceptance of new ways and methods is essential. I believe it is also important to teach traditional Arabic calligraphy when working in Arabic-speaking countries.

Teaching or working in a culture different from your own involves adapting to different social and moral norms, including issues of class and gender. What has your experience been like in these areas, and in what ways did you adapt your working or teaching methods as a result?

I did my PhD on the role of gender in life drawing. The title of my thesis was "From life model to female activist – the double colonization of the female body in Egypt." I had to develop certain methods if I wanted to teach figure drawing, as a naked model would never have been allowed. So I used wire models and anatomy lectures and drawings to teach proportion and movement.

What are the benefits you have gained from working in countries/cultures that are different from your own culture?

I have been back in Germany since 2012 but the Egypt-Germany connection continues. Students still call or write to me if they need my advice. One of them even mentioned me in a TED Talk. I gave a workshop together with a former student at Freie Universität Berlin about Sustainability in Design. My experience is that teaching is not a one-way situation. You give your knowledge and experience and at the same time you get so much back, both emotionally and intellectually.

Fred Meier-Menzel
Studied Communication Design at University of Applied Sciences and Art Hannover, Germany
2006–2012 Design Professor at German University in Cairo, Head of the Drawing Department
2015 Doctorate followed by senior researcher position at Bauhaus University in Weimar, Germany

Agnieszka Ziemiszewska

Workshops: Text Message and Tolerance
The workshops are one of the most important and certainly one of my favorite areas of activity as an educator. The workshop mode makes it possible to look at current issues and to work on them within a short timeframe.

Because workshops usually take place in an environment that is new for the lecturer, they also allow lecturers to look at their own methods from a different perspective. The topics I work on with the participants usually include typography exercises, current problems, or those related to the future, for example, ecology. I think that, in the educational process, it is extremely important to look for inspiration in the world around us. In this way, students not only gain more in-depth knowledge about the subject they are studying, they also learn to carefully observe the world around them and thus broaden their knowledge about themselves. Discussing important and current issues teaches students that they are not only participants but also co-creators of what is here and now.

I have conducted workshops in many countries and, for some of them, I have developed a program so that the activity does not end when the workshop is over. In 2016, we carried out the Text Message project in cooperation with a French university. It explored the issue of how we communicate today. Which explains the title "Text Message." The project (divided into three stages) was attended by more than 100 students from Polish and French universities. Students in Warsaw recorded short video messages that were presented to their French colleagues. French students responded to these messages in the form of a typographic poster. The results were amazing: the authors presented different, often surprising, interpretations of the same message. The project was later shown at an exhi-

5.33 "Text Message" workshop, 2016

bition in Warsaw (as an event accompanying ATypI Warsaw 2016) and in Hebei, China in 2017.

Another program that I also would like to mention is the Tolerance Workshop that I conducted in 2019 at Metropolitan University in Budapest. The topic of tolerance is so extensive that it presents a lot of possibilities for interpretation, but finding the right visual equivalent is not an easy task. Almost every student proposed a different approach, and as they were given the freedom to choose what techniques they would apply to achieve the objective we set at the very beginning, all of the students used a differ-

ent method of implementation. The students found this diversity and surprising combinations of graphic solutions interesting and unusual. But most importantly, the implementation of the topic was accompanied by an interesting and lively discussion. The results of the workshops were evaluated by an international jury that I invited to cooperate, and the best works were shown at Dubai Design Week 2019.

If I was to indicate the most important feature of the workshop program, then I would say that workshops are a form of educational activity in which we engage students rather than tell them what they should do.[14]

5.34 "Tolerance" workshop, 2019

*Please describe your educational background,
including your studies, work/study, and travel.*

I studied Fine Art and Art Education in an interdisciplinary program at the School of the Art
Institute and the University of Illinois at Chicago.
I have lived in Germany since 1981. Since living
in Germany, I have worked as an illustrator,
curator, English teacher, design teacher and as
a fine artist. My art is quite influenced by my
Indian background as well as my US schooling. I have participated in several Berlinales, in
one-woman shows internationally, as well as
other art-related social projects.

*What countries or cultures have you worked and/or
lived in/with extensively or closely? Have you had
formative experiences in other cultures?*

Since I have lived and worked more than ten
years in these areas: Chicago, Cochin, Mumbai,
Berlin and Hamburg, I have deepened my multi-cultural experience even further through language, sound, music and visuals. In my artwork,
I have looked at quests, spirituality, sensuality,
healing, living together, working together,
contrasts, war and children, children in plight,
children on the run, families in fluctuation
and other subjects which delve into how we
humans treat each other.

*What did you know about these countries/cultures
before you started working together?*

I was born in the US, in Chicago, and spent my
early years in India. Since my parents worked as
academics, my cousins and I grew up in India
with our grandmother. When I was eleven years
old, I returned to go to school in my city of birth.
These early influences have made me the artist
a "perpetual immigrant".

I grew up with multiple cultures within cultures,
so I am culturally fluid. This has guided my life
into working as an artist and other professional disciplines. For instance, when I teach classes I get my students to explore their own diversity and what makes them unique, as well as what
they share in common.

*What specific differences have you noticed in how
students learn in other countries/cultures?*

In India the classes within a class-based system
were and are very strict in regard to education.
This is why Indian families and the extended
family push you to compete and excel. However, the US public school system allows space to
explore, or it did in my childhood. So, I was encouraged to draw, to illustrate, to be creative,
which led me to become an artist. In my liber-
al environment, I was viewed as being different.
However, my family was open enough to often
let me be me.

My retrospective is that I have lived and actively
worked in three different education systems: India, USA and Germany. Each learning space has
had different challenges to deal with. A good example of this is when I came to Berlin in 1981
with my young daughter, and she had to adapt to
the German public school system, where natural science and sports are given more space than

creativity and foreign languages. In addition, our American background was preferred to our Indian identity.

Teaching or working in a culture different from your own involves adapting to different social and moral norms, including issues of class and gender. What has your experience been like in these areas, and in what ways did you adapt your working or teaching methods as a result?

I try to get students to use their own biographies to tell their visual stories and acknowledge and embrace their language of imagery. This can cause conflict as moral norms, gender, change, radicalism and class can open and close doors.

Having a multi-cultural background, I don't focus on any limitations, but look for solutions that encourage individuals. My method is to let them tell their own stories, which sensitizes them to barter from perspectives and perceptions that can cross borders.

What are the benefits you have gained from working in countries/ cultures that are different from your own culture?

Seeing people smile and say this has really helped me as well as to deal with the conflicts that come from being unconventional has been rewarding.

I had a drawing class in English where varied ages participated. As an icebreaker, I asked them to sketch the person sitting next to them. So they didn't concentrate on their fear of not being able to draw well, but instead they focused more on communicating with each other. The drawings got better because more confidence and awareness grew. Many were astounded by their results.

Zari Harat
Studied art education and fine arts at
School of the Art Institute of Chicago
Previously High School art teacher in
Chicago/Seattle/San Francisco
Currently art curator, visual artist, art
teacher, designer in Berlin/Hamburg

Sigrid A. Bathke

Studied Social Pedagogy at the Protestant University
of Applied Sciences in Bochum, gained a degree and
PhD in Education from the University of Duisburg-Essen,
Germany
Since 2004, research and consultancy work at the Institut
für soziale Arbeit e.V. (Social Work Institute) in Münster,
Germany
Since 2012, Professor for Social Work in Youth Welfare
at Landshut University, Germany

Learning goal
To become aware of diverging frameworks
of perception and evaluation; making
people more sensitive in dealing with
cultural differences

Theoretical background
Symbolic Interactionism

Teaching method
Visual associations, photo or picture
analysis, structure-laying technique

Associating, understanding and reconstructing
The photo was taken on bali in Indonesia. I discovered this pinkish object against a blue background
while touring. What I really like about this motif are
the colors and the composition. In conceptual terms,
I see my photography in the area of "usual-unusual"
everyday objects or as being inspired by the artistic
style of the 'Objet trouvé'.

Something that is a fascinating peculiarity for the
Western European observer is however often very ba-
nal for a local. My Indonesian guide asked me, "Why
are you photographing a lemonade bag? What's so
special about it?" By comparison, the photo was exhibited in Germany as part of the annual Long Night
of Culture and premiered at the Landshut photo gallery LITVAI in their annual exhibition.

5.35 Just drink, 2017

The reactions and, above all, the associations of Western European colleagues, students and friends were very different to those of people from Asia. The binary nature of "usual-unusual" displayed by the aesthetics of the photo are clearly revealed again and again, and this can be extended towards cultural differences, especially when it comes to understanding cultural systems.[16]

That is why the photo can be used so well in the teaching context when I am trying to raise people's awareness of culturally different allocations of meaning. When the photo is shown to people from Western Europe, their first association is generally with blood or the hospital, they seem to think it has something to do with an infusion. Sometimes it even induces a feeling of disgust. By comparison, when people from Asia and/or from Indonesia see the object in the photo, they immediately identify what it is – namely a plastic bag containing a probably very sugary drink.

I now use the photo all the time in my teaching when the topic is "understanding"[17] and reconstructing the contexts of meaning – for example, in my lectures on qualitative social research.[18] The term "understanding" and reconstructing contexts of meaning is a central element in qualitative social research. When you want to reconstruct and interpret cultural symbols adequately, then the context matters. You must understand this context to be able to correctly interpret what you are seeing. It is, by the way, not necessary when understanding diverging notions to only look at foreign cultures. There are also different "cultures" and milieus in our own countries – just think about the symbolic and language differences between Bavaria and North Rhine-Westphalia. The photo is also useful when I introduce making cultural differences visible in the preparatory seminars for my trips to Indonesia.

On top of that, context-based knowledge that examines ways of life as well as their idiosyncrasies and symbols in a culturally sensitive manner is highly important in other fields of work. Awareness, understanding of and reflection about context-related attributions of meaning are not only vital for people who work in a social profession, but also for creative people or designers, if they want to avoid constant misunderstandings and misinterpretations in their praxis. Without questioning and assessing one's own perspective, which is seen as self-evident and therefore hardly even conscious, interaction and communication are often prematurely given negative connotations or even rejected, as the aforementioned example shows. And yet, intercultural communication is only possible by comparing one's own perception with an understanding of the respective other culture.[19]

When others interpret and assess something very differently in a culture that is not their own, then alien ascriptions result that do not fit in with the everyday reality of the other person's life. There is a risk here that this can lead to people looking down on what is not familiar to them or to stigmatization. The impacts of not understanding properly the everyday reality of a target group's life often leads to a situation where tailormade support that is also accepted by and integrated by the people being addressed cannot be provided. In international teams, the result is ineffective cooperation and frustrated employees. In the design context, thiy may also lead to client dissatisfaction or to products that are unable to achieve their intended impact.[20]

USA ISRAEL THAILAND LOCAL* KOREA

CHINA JAPAN ETHIOPIA RUSSIA EGYPT

6.01 International and local branding

*Traditional German soda called 'Fassbrause'

LOCAL VS. GLOBAL

People have been expressing themselves through design for thousands of years. And they often design things that are merely beautiful, and which have nothing to do with satisfying their basic needs. Beautiful things simply make them happier and more satisfied. This is an ability that sets humans apart from other species.

There are media and designs in our globalized world whose message is understood in almost all cultures. The Coca-Cola word logo is one example. Despite local differences, like the font used, this is recognized wherever you go. It is even understood in Chinese symbols for those who are foreign to Chinese culture because of its four syllables – Co-ca Co-la – and because of its typography and color. It is interesting that the design of the product advertising functions globally in a more uniform manner than the product content. Although it is a globally operating corporation, Coca-Cola pursues a local design strategy. The recipes are adapted to the taste preferences of the consumers.[1] The sugar content in Fanta Orange varies from country to country. In Germany, it is 45.5g, in France only 32.5g per half liter, for example. The color and flavors are also different in different countries. Because of color preferences, Fanta Orange in Thailand has a much stronger orange tone than in Germany. In Indonesia there is a strawberry flavor, which is far more popular there than orange.[2]

Tastes are different. They are individual and – no matter whether for soft drinks or effective posters – they are socio-culturally influenced. Design also reflects cultural identity and is never unpolitical or ahistorical. Design as a cultural characteristic makes a considerable contribution towards building, securing and presenting a community's identity.[3] Designers are ambassadors of cultural identity and have a responsibility as such. They translate and communicate their culture and create something new at the same time. In this way, they make sure that their local cultural heritage is not overcome by global elements, and that it does not disappear. This securing of local identity, remembering and differentiating, is becoming increasingly difficult in a globalized world. And that is why UNESCO has decided to promote an awareness of cultural heritage at local and national level.[4]

The following tells the local design history of three countries on different continents. Cuba's design history shows the result of decades of political isolation, Poland's that of a tradition of financial independence, and Indonesia's reveals a post-colonial cultural mix that seeks to preserve its traditional roots.

Cuba

For a long time, design played a subordinate role in Cuba. In pre-revolutionary Cuba (1902-1958), the neo-colonialists were not interested in promoting creative, never mind political, forms of expression. There are, however, a few examples of design that are known today, such as tobacco labels, which can be seen as the oldest packaging creations on the Caribbean island, and which bring together in a memorable manner the design and culture of the country.

Altogether, Cuba has struggled over hundreds of years against numerous dictators and for its independence. This struggle ended for some decades following the revolution at the end of the 1950s. After that, the faces of the revolutionary heroes Fidel Castro and Che Guevara could be found on countless posters and became just as popular as the posters of pop singers.[5] After the revolution, Cuban design moved away from advertising content and towards educational, cultural and political messages. Posters became a form of mass media. The forefathers of the classic Cuban poster originate from this period. At the beginning of the 1980s, publications like *Prisma*, *Revolución y Cultura* and *Cuba Internacional* presented the current poster art and had some formal and typographic successes. The first and only university design center in Cuba, ISDI (Higher Institute of Industrial Design), was set up in 1984.[6]

At the end of the 1990s, the Cuban economic crisis caused by the fall of the socialist bloc led to radical change and disillusionment in Cuban poster art. This period was a setback for all of Cuban art, because survival and satisfying people's basic needs took utmost priority. The result was a lull in creativity in Cuban design. Some works that were meaningful in a Cuban and international context, however, were collected in the poster club CACa (Club de Amigos del Cartel) and elsewhere. All of this happened in a time in which the first generation of Cuban designers had just graduated from the ISDI. However, there was hardly any commercial work, and designers tended to show their work in competitions and exhibitions.[7]

The 2000s saw a revival of poster art and it has since played an important role in the country's cultural heritage. In the homage by Edel Rodríguez to the most famous Cuban musician Bola de Nieve (Bola en su centenario, 2011) or in the homage by Michelle Mijares (Memorias del Subdesarrollo) on the 40th anniversary of the film, graphics are presented with concepts that show and preserve cinema and music as inseparable components of Cuba's national identity. These homages use a bold language made up of cartoon, chromatic elements and symbols that present the object of typography. They have become a visual message that communicates the Cuban way of life.[8]

6.02 Ball celebrating the 100th anniversary, 2011

6.03 Havana World Music Festival, 2016

Edel Rodríguez Mola, Cuba

Edel Rodríguez Mola, born in 1982 in Havana, Cuba, heralded in a new era of graphic design from the end of the 1990s until shortly after the beginning of the 2000s together with Giselle Monzón and other graduates of Cuba's design university, the Higher Institute of Industrial Design (ISDI). He became famous for his poster for the 100th anniversary of Cuba's most famous musician of the 20th century, Bola de Nieve. He is the recipient of many prizes, for example, the Best Poster Design 2013 by Havana's Club of Friends of the Poster (CACA).

6.04 Medea, 2013

6.05 Dogs that never barked, 2012

Indania del Río, Cuba

Indania del Río, born in 1981, is a Cuban designer and graphic
designer. She attended the Instituto Superior de Diseño Industrial in
Havana, where she gained her degree in Graphic Design and Visual
Communication in 2004. Her poster art has been shown in Cuban
and international exhibitions, among these the Seattle-Havana
Poster Show 2007-2008 and in the exhibitions Ghost Posters 2009
and Últimas Escenas 2011. In 2015, she opened the first independently
managed Cuban design store Clandestina in Old Havana with her
Spanish business partner Leire Fernández.

Giselle Monzón, Cuba

Giselle Monzón, born in Villa Clara, Cuba in 1979, is a graphic designer and graduated from the Institute for Design (ISDI). She designs posters for theaters, the visual arts and films. She has won the Coral Grand Prize in the Poster category twice at the International Festival, and she was a finalist in various international poster biennials. She has participated in exhibitions in Cuba, Switzerland and the EU and works as a professor at the Cuban Higher Design Institute and the Communications Faculty at the University of Havana.

6.06 Poster for the 10th anniversary of the poster biennial of Bolivia, 2018

6.07 Movie poster "7 Días en La Habana" by various directors, 2011

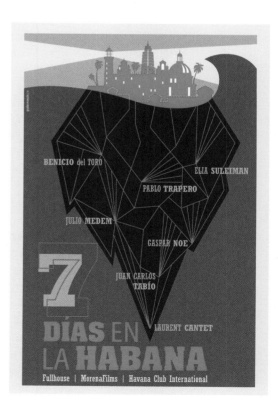

Poland

At the end of the 19th century, Kraków established itself as the cradle of artistic and scientific life in modern Poland. Color lithography had just been invented, the idea of the poster had been born in France, and Henri de Toulouse-Lautrec was a celebrated artist. It was in this environment that the Polish poster appeared. These were art-related or used to announce exhibitions, for example. In 1898, the 1st international poster exhibition took place in Kraków. Even at this time, Polish posters stood out due to their high artistic quality and their interesting style mix of art nouveau, cubism and folklore.[9]

The demand for poster advertising was great after World War One, and students of architecture were very proficient at creating effective advertising posters. They had little difficulty in using the rules of geometry and proportions they had learned for commercial purposes. They adapted their style to suit the respective poster topic – humorous displayed dance-like, and dynamic showed sporting.[10]

Following World War Two, the Polish poster was given a new aesthetic look and was mainly used as propaganda material. The posters were marked by socialist realism, and the first studio for propaganda posters was set up in Lublin.

In the 1950s, imagination and drawing quality once again came into focus. "Art advertises art" was the motto. The film and exhibition posters of the young artists not only announced, but communicated in equal measure.[11] Film Polski and the Center for Film Distribution were the main clients. The poster was now the only form of individual artistic expression that was permitted, and the state did not censor posters like it did other media. What is more, the art and design sector was state subsidized. Artists could develop their creative work free from the constraints of the market. This was the birth of the "School of the Polish Poster Art[12]". Because it was not bound by stylistic or commercial restraints, poster art was humorous, irreverent, free and intellectually demanding.[13] It was not ruled by either Hollywood or the market.[14] Famous figures in this scene included Henryk Tomaszewski and Jan Lenica. In reviews, Lenica's posters were referred to, for example, as "socialist realism on LSD".[15] The color schemes were expressive, objects joined up to make fantastical forms.

The 1980s saw strong opposition to the increasingly repressive Communist Party. Poster art witnessed a decline, as other things like financial survival became more important. New work for artists did not come until privatization. Today there are independent poster artists who are aware of their heritage, are internationally known and use a variety of styles and perspectives.

6.08 Freedom, 2014

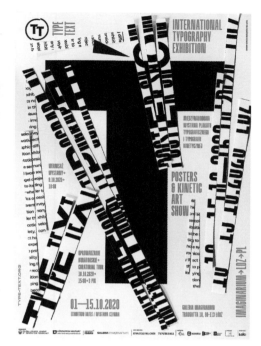

6.09 Type Text Identity, 2020

Agnieszka Ziemiszewska, Poland

Agnieszka Ziemiszewska is a graphic designer, academic lecturer and curator. She received her master's from the Faculty of Graphic Art at the Academy of Fine Art in Łódź and her PhD from the Academy of Fine Art in Warsaw. She works as a Professor at the typography studio of the Polish-Japanese Institute for Information Technology in Warsaw, and she gives workshops and lectures in Poland, China and France, among others. She has been awarded several prizes, including the Platinum Award at the Creativity Annual Awards in the USA, and received a grant from the Polish Ministry for Culture and National Heritage.

6.10 Adele has not had supper yet, 2019

Jerzy Skakun and Joanna Górska, Poland
Jerzy Skakun and Joanna Górska are graduates of the Painting
Faculty at Academy of Fine Arts in Gdańsk. In their graphic design
studio, Homework, established in 2003, they design posters and
printed graphics for cultural events and institutions like the National
Museum in Warsaw and the Museum of the History of Polish Jews.
They have received a number of awards, including the Gold Medal in
2008 at the Poster Biennial in Mexico and the 2017 Grant Front for
the best Polish cover in the category "Politics, Business and Society".

6.11 Concert Liban, 2017

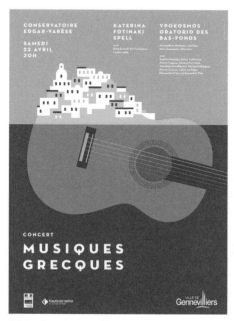

6.12 Greek music concert, 2017

6.13 Tango festival, 2017

6.14 BEM! Musical play poster, 2018

Marcin Władyka, Poland

Marcin Władyka was born in Warsaw in 1975. He studies at the School of Design in St. Gallen, Switzerland and studied his MA in 1999 from the Academy of Fine Arts in Warsaw. In the same year, he set up his own design studio HEADMADE. Since 2000, he has been working as a lecturer for Poster Design, Publishing Design, Typography and Motion Design at the Academy of Fine Art and various art schools in Warsaw. In 2012, he completed his PhD in Publishing Design and, since 2016, he has been giving MA classes at the Polish-Japanese Academy for Information Technology.

6.15 Poster for an exhibition of Piotr Siwczuk, 2003

6.16 Escape from the Polish Cinema, play poster, 2017

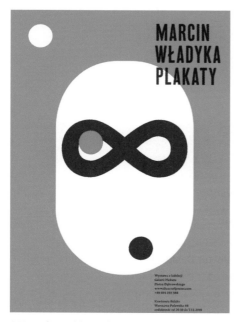

6.17 Poster for an exhibition of Piotr Dabrowski, 2018

6.18 Dymny, play poster, 2019

Please describe your educational background, including your studies, work/study, and travel.

I studied at the Academy of Fine Arts in Łódź, which has a very rich tradition in typography. After graduating, I spent many years working as a graphic designer. At some point, I realized that working only on commercial projects was not very progressive for me, so I decided to start my Ph.D. at the Academy of Fine Arts in Warsaw. In contrast to my previous typography-oriented Academy in Łódź, this was a new experience based on the traditions of the Polish School of Poster Art.

In later years, when I was presenting my achievements in lectures, I often titled them: Between Word and Image. The word was a symbolic reference to Łódź and its most important intangible traditions (typography), and the image was a reference to Warsaw (illustration, Polish School of Poster Art). Between seems to be the most appropriate term to describe the extremely fascinating area that I discovered for myself as a huge and endless source of inspiration.

Once I was an experienced designer, I started my academic career and decided to reduce the amount of commercial work I did. Currently, I am a professor at the Polish-Japanese Academy of Information Technology and the Academy of Fine Arts in Warsaw. I often invite my colleagues from other countries to work together and share experiences. I am curious and interested in the world and in people. I have visited many countries and continents, not only for professional purposes, and I am still fascinated by the diversity of the world.

What countries or cultures have you worked and/or lived in/with extensively or closely? Have you had formative experiences in other cultures?

I have conducted workshops and lectures in France, Bulgaria, China, Hungary, the Netherlands, Indonesia, South Korea and Germany, Jordan, Arab Emirates, and Iran. Most of them had a weekly or biweekly mode.

During the pandemic, I conducted online workshops for 40 students from China. Although I have been to China previously this proved to be an extraordinary experience of communication without the possibility of personal contact. However, it can also be said that it was the most personal contact that I have ever had with the students, because my Chinese students hosted me at their homes. I had a chance to see not only their workplace but also to witness how proudly they shared the progress of their designs with members of their families. It was a very enriching experience, not only in terms of communication and education.

What did you know about these countries/cultures before you started working together?

When I get an invitation to lead workshops in a country that I haven't visited before, I do basic research regarding the specifics of a place. I also have many friends abroad, so there is always an opportunity to learn about the place from sources other than just data contained in publications or on the Internet.

If I have a lecture or presentation, I try to prepare at least a fragment of it in the language of the host country.

What specific differences have you noticed in how students learn in other countries/cultures?

Despite some differences, I believe that in a way we are all very similar to each other. We all need attention, mutual respect, and understanding even beyond languages. Although I do not like generalizations, If I were to point to a common factor, it would certainly be that all the students I met knew about the Polish School of Poster Art, and they described it as wonderful inspiration.

Teaching or working in a culture different from your own involves adapting to different social and moral norms, including issues of class and gender. What has your experience been like in these areas, and in what ways did you adapt your working or teaching methods as a result?

I believe that graphic design is not only about creating beautiful images but also about shaping good manners and culture in a wider aspect. I try to spread this idea by also taking up the topics of tolerance or equal rights. If I know that in a country there are customs that reflect a certain style of clothing or other traditions, I simply respect the habits of the host.

What are the benefits you have gained from working in countries/cultures that are different from your own culture?

The most important benefit is the opportunity to encounter new people, cultures, places. Sometimes these are surprising meetings, always very informative. I often say that I learn more from my students than they learn from me.

In almost every country people have difficulty pronouncing my name and surname. During my stay in China, I got an email titled professor Aka. I realized that Chinese people invented a way to solve this problem. That was a great lesson on how to simplify communication. I found this solution extremely inventive and helpful in my communications and since then I ask my students to just call me that.

Agnieszka Ziemiszewska
Studied at Academy of Fine Arts
in Łódź, Poland
Ph.D at Academy of Fine Arts in Warsaw.
Professor at the Polish-Japanese
Academy of Information Technology and
at the Academy of Fine Arts in Warsaw.
Teaching expertise and exhibitions:
USA, China, Italy, Germany, Taiwan,
Japan, Bolivia, Russia, Iran, among others
Awards: Creativity Annual Awards (USA),
Grand Prix der Polish Poster Biennial,
among others

Indonesia

In its initial phases, Indonesian graph-ic design was very much influenced by the foreign ideas and values of the colo-nial rulers and occupiers. They not only brought their concepts to the economy of the island state, but also to its design and advertising sectors. The Dutch coloni-alists imported book printing in the 17th century in order to distribute official an-nouncements and missionary tractates.[16] The first advertising agency was founded in 1917 by Chinese people and, from 1905 onwards, the Aneta[17] news agency existed with its advertising department whose employees came from Europe.

The first art school was established in 1947 by the Dutch colonial government at Bandung Institute of Technology (ITB). As always, its visual language was domi-nated by the Dutch influence. Restaurant adverts, for example, showed an illustra-tion of an Indonesian waiter in a white suit with a traditional hat taking orders from a Dutch customer.[18] Many Indonesians were illiterate, with the rate of illiteracy in the population still at around 67% in 1980.[19] This meant that people had to clearly rec-ognize what was being advertised. The local advertising agency Inter-Visa Ltd. – a pioneer of modern advertising – was set up in 1967. 1980 saw the establishment of the Indonesian Graphic Design Society (IPGI), today the ADGI.[20]

In 1984, several art disciplines were com-bined together in what became Indonesia's other important art and design academy, the Indonesian Institute of the Arts

(Institut Seni Indonesia or ISI) in Yogyakarta, whose predecessor (ASRI) had already been founded in 1949 as the first state art school in the still young Republic of Indonesia.

At the changeover to the new millenni-um, computer and communications tech-nologies elevated advertising and graph-ic design to a new level. Hundreds of new magazines were published, such as the *Cakram* graphic design magazine.[21]

Today, Indonesia is in the process of dis-covering its own path in graphic design in a fusion of global influences and tra-ditional techniques like Batik. "It is a bal-ancing act that tries to preserve its own roots,"[22] John Kudos wrote. Western prod-ucts and designs still command a great deal of respect and the post-colonial in-fluence can be seen above all in advertis-ing for cosmetics like the products used to lighten skin tone.[23]

There are currently three design orienta-tions in Indonesia: 1. Commercial design, which is influenced by the USA (tobacco), Korea (social media), Singapore, China and the Arab countries.[24] 2. Communica-tions design, especially corporate identity media, that have a sleek, professional style and can hardly be differentiated from their Western counterparts. 3. Experimental graphic design that, among other things, is seen in cultural posters and comics. Comic posters, like those by Apotik, bring together familiar stories with humor in order to encourage people to think about things and change their perspective.[25]

6.19 IF Film Festival New York, 2019

John Kudos, Indonesia

John Kudos completed his general school education in Bandung, Indonesia, and he studied at the Maryland Institute College of Art from 2001. Following that, he worked for seven years at Pentagram in New York with Abbott Miller. In 2008, he set up Kudos Design Collaboratory in New York. The agency works with forward-looking brands and institutions to develop brandings, UX- and Interaction Design, Editorial Design, and Environmental Graphic Design. It has received numerous awards. Kudos also teaches at the Maryland Institute College of Art, the School of Visual Arts, The New School, and Cornell University.

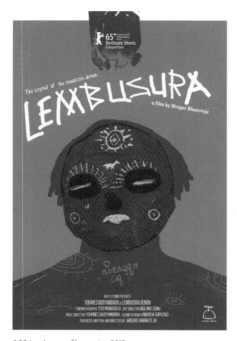

6.20 Lembusura, film poster, 2015

6.21 Prenjak, film poster, 2016

Studio Batu, Indonesia

Studio Batu – a multi-disciplinary, Indonesian collective – was founded in 2013. It is made up of artists from the fields of film, music, design and architecture. Their film "Lembusura" won a prize at the 2014 Berlinale and "In the Year of Monkey" took an award at Cannes in 2016. Studio Batu uses a mix of platforms such as puppets, light, shade and 2D mapping to express themselves artistically. In 2019, with the support of the Djarum Foundation, they created the performance "While You're Away" along with "Your Tail is Red" with the support of Yayasan Kelola. Their work focuses on the topics of love, tragedy, ideology and otherness.

Indieguerillas, Indonesia

Indieguerillas was set up in 1999 by the artist couple Santi Ariestyowanti (communications designer) and Dyatmiko "Miko" Bawono (interior designer) from Yogyakarta, Indonesia. Both are graduates of the Faculty of Art at the Indonesian Institute of the Arts in Yogyakarta. The Indieguerillas are internationally known for their interest in everyday and design culture, and for their colorful intermedia experiments that are fully in tune with the zeitgeist in a constantly changing urban culture. They create spatial installations with imaginary creatures that are often taken from Indonesian culture. They are part of the international art scene.

6.22 Lompat Besar (Big Leap), Installation, 2015
6.23 Panjang Umrur, Picture, 2019

6.24 Kawan Korupsi, 2015

6.25 Campaign for the HIV AIDS
Global Fund (RED), 2006

Please describe your educational background, including your studies, work/study, and travel.

I'm a graphic designer and hiker. I graduated in Graphic Design from the Institut Teknologi Bandung Art and Design School in Indonesia in 1997. It was one of the country's first graphic design schools, influenced by Dutch designers like Gert Dumbar and Jan Van Toorn from Maastricht's Jan Van Eyck Academie. I went to New York in 1998, graduating with a Master's in Communication Design in 2000. In my free time I hike, camp and travel with my family. I'm now a creative director at BARK&Co in New York City.

What countries or cultures have you worked and/or lived in/with extensively or closely? Have you had formative experiences in other cultures?

I was born in Bandung, Indonesia. Friends who were art directors or copywriters in advertising sometimes asked me for help on specific campaigns, to help powerful brands deliver a message and story to the community. It required true awareness and understanding of the local culture of the target groups. In 2015, my friend Elwin Mok (Head of Indonesia Advertising Association in Jakarta) asked me to design a national campaign for Seni Lawan Korupsi (art vs. corruption) for the Jakarta Arts Council. As an Indonesian graphic designer living in NY, I am familiar with Indonesia's symbols and metaphors of corruption, and the way of creating juxtapositions using local words (Bahasa). This campaign created an ironic but provoking logotype transforming KAWAN (to befriend) vigorously into LAWAN (to fight), and creating a short serial animation turning the local symbol of corruption (rats) into a pirate bomb explosion.

What did you know about these countries/cultures before you started working together?

I knew a lot from friends working in advertising throughout South-East Asia and in the US.

Henri Kusbiantoro
Studied at ITB School of Art and Design in Bandung, Indonsien and at Pratt Institute, New York
Associate creative director at FutureBrand, New York, design director at Siegel+Gale, New York, etc. Since 2020 Associate creative director at BARK&Co, New York
Awards: Transform Awards, Rebrand 100, GRAPHIS Design Annual, New York Art Director Club etc.

What specific differences have you noticed in how students learn in other countries/cultures?

Differences can be seen as obstacles. But students should see them as strengths, as enriching and surprising opportunities. When studying at Pratt, I observed two different cultures or countries to discover their similar approach (not just differences) to solving a problem with a different execution and style. The result was mind-blowing. My 1999 MFA thesis focused on developing a symbiotic approach between the Swiss international grid system in graphic design layout and Indonesia's pattern system in Batik layout. Surprisingly, these two different methods and approaches can transform into new languages of graphic design and be used to develop bespoke fonts. The thesis was demonstrated visually and simulated at the EXPO 2000 in Hannover.

Teaching or working in a culture different from your own involves adapting to different social and moral norms, including issues of class and gender. What has your experience been like in these areas, and in what ways did you adapt your working or teaching methods as a result?

You experience different sides of New York when you arrive there. As a tourist, you might find its extraordinary energy a bit chaotic — constant police and rats in the subway stations. But if you study and work there, you discover a love and hate that grows slowly. You learn to like bagels and cheese spread and live with subway delays in the morning, find the most impressive Chinese literature and roof architecture collections outside Beijing at the Metropolitan Museum of Art in the afternoon. Then, at night, hang out with friends from all different ethnicities, genders and backgrounds at the yakitori place in St. Marks Place, as authentic as

anything in Tokyo. It's a process and journey over years and it forms a new perspective, mind and soul.

Involving and adapting cultures in your design and work process becomes an essential challenge and, by default, it is the key and habit of success in every project to explore unbiased solutions, richer approaches and unshaken results.

What are the benefits you have gained from working in countries/cultures that are different from your own culture?

When you can laugh at yourself without being defensive, without being sensitive due to your cultural pride or background, you're not just on the right track but surpassing the finish line.

6.26 Campaign for the HIV AIDS
Global Fund (RED), 2006

6.27 Batik and Brockmann
(Master thesis), EXPO 2000
Hannover, 1999

CHAPTER 1 | SIGNS

1   **Meier-Oeser, Stephan (2011):** *Medieval Semiotics.*
    URL: https://plato.stanford.edu/entries/semiotics-medieval [08.12.2020].

2   **Eco, Umberto (1967):** *A Theory of Semiotics (Advances in Semiotics).*

3   **Watzlawick P., Beavin J. B., Jackson D. D. (1967):** *Pragmatics of Human Communication: A Study of Interactional Patterns, Pathologies and Paradoxes, 1st ed., p. 51.*

4   **Schulz von Thun, Friedemann (2016):** *Miteinander reden Kommunikationspsychologie für Führungskräfte.*

5   **Saussure, Ferdinand de (1994):** *Course in General Linguistics.*

6   **Houser N./Kloesel C. J. W. (ed.) (1983):** *The Essential Peirce,* Volume 1 and 2: *Selected Philosophical Writings.*

7   **Ogden C. K., Richards I. A. (1923):** *The Meaning of Meaning.*

8   **Morris, Charles W. (1946):** *Signs, Language and Behavior.*

CHAPTER 2 | BASIC ELEMENTS AND BASIC FORMS

1   **Chokron, S. and De Agostini, M. (2000):** *Reading habits influence aesthetic preference.*
    in: Cognitive Brain Research Volume 10, Issues 1–2, September 2000, pp. 45-49.

2   **Friedrich, Trista E., Elias, Lorin J. (2016):** *The write bias: The influence of native writing direction on aesthetic preference biases,* in: Psychology of Aesthetics, Creativity, and the Arts, Vol 10(2), S. 128-133.

3   **Max Wertheimer (1880–1943)** is regarded as the main founder of Gestalt psychology. In 1923 he formulated the Gestalt laws such as the law of proximity, the good Gestalt and the law of unity. These have maintained their significance for designers right up to the present day. The German word "Gestalt" found its way into the English language in World War II via the Jewish diaspora and is explained in the Cambridge Dictionary as follows: *"Something such as a structure or experience that, when considered as a whole, has qualities that are more than the total of all its parts."* This picks up on the sentence, said to come from Aristoteles: *"The whole is more than the sum of its parts."* What all the different psychological approaches have in common is that they are all about wholeness. You can imagine this in the design of a smiley. It consists only of a semicircle (mouth) and two circles (eyes). The individual parts have no meaning in themselves, and only make sense as a whole. If you change one part of it, the entire statement changes.

4   **Blakemore, C. and Cooper, G. F.** published their research results on the early development of the brain in cats in 1970. They proved that the development of the brain is dependent on the visual environment.

5   **Kandinsky, Wassily (1926):** *Point and Line to Plane* (Punkt und Linie zu Fläche), vol. 9 of the Bauhaus Books, reprint in 7th ed., 1955, p. 167; English translation published 1947 by Solomon R. Guggenheim Foundation New York.

6   **David Hubel and Torsten Wiesel** received the Nobel Prize in 1981 for their research work on information processing in the visual system.

7   **Wolfgang Köhler** proved in an experiment in 1929 that language and visual images are connected. He used the word pair "Takete-Maluma". The majority of the test subjects assigned Takete a pointed form and Maluma a soft, round form. In 2001, sound-shape mapping was once again proved using the word pair "Bouba-Kiki". This sound symbolism also works in small children and interculturally, but only when the sound structure already exists in the respective language.

8   **Kandinsky, Wassily (1926):** *"Dance Curves: The Dances of Palucca",* Das Kunstblatt, Potsdam, vol. 10, no. 3, pp. 117-21.

9   **Golomb, Claire (2004):** *The Child's Creation of a Pictorial World,* 2nd ed., p. 15, p. 12

10 **See Verstockt, Mark (1987):** *The Genesis of Form: From Chaos to Geometry,* pp. 85—95.

11 **Bill, Max (1957):** *Die gute Form,* Winterthur.

12 **Lupton, Ellen (2009):** *Graphic Design Theory, Reading from the Field,* pp. 64—69 and pp. 90—93, New York.

13 **The animated film Logorama (2009),** shows an urban and stylized cityscape that exists of nothing but advertising surfaces and logos, taking Los Angeles as an example. Even the characters in the film are based on brands like Esso and Michelin. The short film won an Oscar in 2010.

14 **Rob Janoff,** the designer of the Apple logo said in an interview: *"He (Steve Jobs) just smiled and nodded and didn't say much"*, URL: https://www.logodesignlove.com/rob-janoff-apple-logo-designer, [23.02.2021].

CHAPTER 3 | TYPE AND FORM

1 **Joordens, J./d'Errico, F./ Wesselingh, F. et al. (2015):** *Homo erectus at Trinil on Java used shells for tool production and engraving*, in: Nature 518, p. 228-231, doi: 10.1038/nature13962.

2 **Aubert, M./ Lebe, R./ Oktaviana, A. et al. (2019):** *Earliest hunting scene in prehistoric art,* in: Nature. 576, p. 442-445, doi: 10.1038/s41586-019-1806-y.

3 **Weisdorf, Jacob L. (2005):** *From Foraging To Farming. Explaining The Neolithic Revolution*, in: Journal of Economic Survey, Vol. 19, issue 4, S. 563-564/574-578.

4 **Fay, N./Ellison, T. M./Garrod, S. (2014):** *Iconicity. From Sign to System in Human Communication and Language,* in: Pragmatics & Cognition 22, S. 245, doi: 10.1075/pc.22.2.05fay.

5 **Puhvel, Jaan (2019):** *Cuneiform*, URL: https://www.britannica.com/topic/cuneiform [23.02.2021].

6 **Houston, Stephen D. (2004):** *The First Writing. Script Invention as History and Process.*

7 **Eberhard, D. M./ Simons, G. F./ Fennig, C. D. (Hg.) (2020):** *Ethnologue: Languages of the World,* URL: https://www.ethnologue.com/enterprise-faq/how-many-languages-world-are-unwritten-0 [23.02.2021].

8 **Valentino, Andrea (2020):** *The alphabets at risk of extinction,* URL: https://www.bbc.com/future/article/20200121-the-alphabets-at-risk-of-extinction [23.02.2021].

9 **McLuhan, Marshall (1962):** *The Gutenberg Galaxy. The making of typographic ma*n, S. 13/ 36/ 55.

10 **Grady, C. L./McIntosh, A. R. et. al. (1989):** *Neural correlates of the episodic encoding of pictures and words, in: Proceedings of the National Academy of Sciences,* Vol. 95, S. 2705, doi: 10.1073/pnas.95.5.2703.

11 **Clayton, Ewan (o. J.):** *A short history of calligraphy and typography,* URL: https://www.bl.uk/history-of-writing/articles/a-short-history-of-calligraphy-and-typography [23.02.2021].

12 **The font provider MyFonts** has more than 100,000 individual fonts such as regular, bold and italic on offer. Adobe's Creative Suite has more than 2,000 font families, which include different weights and styles and Google Fonts even offers more than 1,000 families free of charge.

13 **The fractured scripts like Gothic** (from the 12th century) are not considered, as they are hardly used today.

14 **Radtke, S. P./Pisani, P./ Wolters, W. (2013):** *Handbuch Visuelle Mediengestaltung,* 7th edition, p. 152-167.

15 **Alliance of German Designers (AGD) e.V.,** URL:https://agd.de/wp-content/uploads/2015/01/agd-weidemann-plakat-hoch.pdf [23.02.2021].

16 **Pentagram** has existed for more than 50 yeas and ist the biggest independent and owner-managed design agency worldwide with studios in New York, Berlin and London.

17 **Type foundry:** Audi Type by the Dutch type foundry Bold Monday, BBC Reith Sans and Serif by Dalton Maag and TCCC Unity for Coca-Cola by Neville Brody.

18 **Bantjes, Marian (2013):** *Pretty Pictures,* p. 83

19 **Literature: Healy, John F. (1990):** *Reading the Past. The Early Alphabet.* / **Mioni, Elpidio (1977):** *Introduzione alla Paleografia Greca.* / **Scholderer, Victor (1994):** *Greek Printing Types.* / **Macrakis, Michael S. (ed.) (1996):** *Greek Letters. From Tablets to Pixels.* / **"Athens / Αθήνα" (2017/18):** *Typography & Graphic Design.* / **Matthiopoulos, Georgios D. (2019):** *Ανθολογία της ελληνικής τυπογραφίας* (An illustrated Anthology of Greek Typography). / **Greek Font Society,** URL: https://www.greekfontsociety-gfs.gr [23.02.2021].

20 **Literature: Liu, Eric (2019):** *Collection of Research on Chinese Typography* 中文字设计研究选集 / **URL:** https://www.thetype.com/shop-2/collection [23.02.2021]. / **Reed, Christopher A. (2014):** *Gutenberg in Shanghai. Chinese Print Capitalism (1876-1937)* 古登堡在上海海：中国印刷资本主义. / **Zhou, Bo (2018):** *History of Chinese Modern Character Design* 中国现代文文字设计图史 / **Zhou, B./ Wu, F./Liu, C. (2017):** Chinese Type Modern 字体摩登 / **Jiang, Q./ Liu. R. (2014):** *Shanghai Characters* 上海海字记 / **Sun, Mingyuan (2018):** *Juzhen's Study of Song Style* 聚珍仿宋体研究

21   Literature: AbiFarès, Huda Smitshuijzen (2002): *Arabic Typography: A Comprehensive Sourcebook.*
     'Azab, K./Hasan M. (2011): *Diwan al-khatt al-'arabi fi Misr: dirasa watha'iqiya li-l-kitabat wa-ahamm al-khattatin fi 'asr
     usrat Muhammad 'Ali.* Alexandria: Maktabat al-Iskandariya li-l-Nashr wa-l-Tawzi', 2011. / **Blair, Sheila S (2006):** *Islamic
     Calligraphy.* / **Hamm, Roberto** (1975): *Pour une Typographie Arabe* (For an Arab Typography) / **Milo, Thomas (2002):**
     Arabic Script and Typography. A Brief Historical Overview. In John D. Berry, ed., Language Culture Type. International
     type design in the age of Unicode, 112-27. / **Shehab, Bahia, and Haytham Nawar (2020):** *A History of Arab Graphic
     Design.* / Zoghbi, Pascal. "Beyond Latin." Eye, 2015.

CHAPTER 4 | COLOR

1   Schläpfer, K. K. (2012): *Möglichkeiten zur Erweiterung des Farbraums*, in: Jahrbuch 2012 Verein deutscher Druck-
      ingenieure e.V., p. 41.

2   Sun, X. (2009): *Connecting Heaven and Man. The role of astronomy in ancient Chinese society and culture*, in:
      The Role of Astronomy in Society and Culture Proceedings IAU Symposium No. 260, p. 99.

3   Littlejohn, R. (year not given): Wuxing (Wu-hsing), in: *The Internet Encyclopedia of Philosophy.* URL: https://iep.utm.
      edu/wuxing [23.02.2021].

4   Huiqin, Z. (2014): *On Confucianism reflected in the description of clothing in the Analects of Confucius*, in:
      The Research Journal of the Costume Culture Vol.22, No.6, pp.1028-1033.

5   Hu, Xiaoyan Hu (2016): *The Notion of 'Qi Yun' (Spirit Consonance) in Chinese Painting*, in: Proceedings of the
      European Society for Aesthetics Volume 8, p. 249.

6   Kirchner, E. (2015): *Color theory and color order in medieval Islam. A review*, in: Wiley Periodicals, Vol. 40, pp. 5-16.

7   For acrylic paititng, Betty Edwards recommends the following seven basic colors: Cadmium yellow pale, Cadmium
      orange, Cadmium red medium, Alizarin crimson, Cobalt violet, ultramarine blue, permanent green and Titanium
      white and Ivory black, in: Edwards, Betty (2004): Color. A course in mastering the art of mixing color, p. 37.

8   Albers, J. (2013): *Interaction of color.*

9   Dittmann, L. (2003): *Die Farbtheorie Johannes Ittens*, in: *Beiträge eines wissenschaftlichen Symposiums*, pp. 178-208.

10   Itten, Johannes (1961): *Kunst der Farbe.*

11   The hashtag #sunset occupies 45th place on Instagram and is named in fourth place in the Nature section, preceded
      only by #Nature, #Summer and #Dog. Cf. URL: https://top-hashtags.com/instagram/ [23.02.2021]

12   Buether, Axel (2020): *Die geheimnisvolle Macht der Farben.* Kindl-Version, German Edition. Pos. 830: "Warme Farben
      wie Rot, Orange und Gelb treten in den Vordergrund, während kalte wie Blau und Türkis zurückweichen." Pos. 1650:
      "Blau hat den Charakter einer Lichtfarbe, die uns Räume öffnet und aufgrund ihrer Immaterialität keine Gefahr
      darstellt. Es gibt daher keine andere Farbe, der wir intuitiv mehr vertrauen."

13   Kay, P./Berlin, B./Maffi, L./ Merrifield, W. R./Cook, R. (2020): *The World Color Survey, Center for the Study of Language
      and Information*, 2nd edition.

14   Deutscher, Guy (2010): *Through The Language Glass. Why The World Looks Different In Other Languages.*

15   Kay, P./Berlin, B./Maffi, L./ Merrifield, W. R./Cook, R (1969): *The World Color Survey.*

16   Mehta, R./Zhu, R. (2009): *Blue or Red? Exploring the Effect of Color on Cognitive Task Performances*, Science 27, Vol. 323,
      Issue 5918, pp. 1226-1229. URL: https://science.sciencemag.org/content/323/5918/1226 [23.02.2021].

17   URL: https://www.sciencemag.org/news/2017/05/babies-gazes-suggest-we-are-born-understanding-color
      [23.02.2021].

18   URL: https://wisotop.de/warum-sehen-wir-farben.php [23.02.2021].

19   Reinhard, Wolfgang (2004): *Lebensformen Europas. Eine historische Kulturanthropologie*, p. 128.

20   Han, J./Quye, A. (2018): *Dyes and Dyeing in the Ming and Qing Dynastiesin China. Preliminary Evidence Based on
      Primary Sources of Documented Recipes*, in: Textile History, Volume 48, S. 2. URL: http://eprints.gla.ac.
      uk/157138/7/157138.pdf [23.02.2021].

21 **Irtem, Çiğdem (2014):** *Osmanli Kültüründe Renk Kavrami ve Sosyal Yapiya Etkilieri.* URL: http://earsiv.halic.edu.tr/xmlui/bitstream/handle/20.500.12473/619/385749.pdf?sequence=1 [23.02.2021].

22 **Elliot, Matthew (2004):** *Dress Codes in the Ottoman Empire.* The Case of the Franks, in: Ottoman Costumes: From Textile to Identity, pp. 105-107.

23 **Thurn, Hans Peter (2007):** *Farbwirkungen. Soziologie der Farbe,* p. 18. ff.

24 **Jonauskaite, D./Abdel-Khalek, A. M./Abu-Akel, A., et al. (2019):** *The sun is no fun without rain:* Physical environments affect how we feel about yellow across 55 countries, in: Journal of Environmental Psychology 66, 101350, p. 6.

25 **Hårleman, Maud (2007):** *Daylight Influence on Colour Design:* Empirical Study on Perceived Colour and Colour Experience Indoors, p. 46.

26 **Müller, Stefan (2020):** *Interkulturelles Marketing,* p. 293.

27 **Michiels, Inez (2018):** *Indications for a Valid Color Test to Measure Personality, Visual Needs and Preferences for Tailored Design Applications,* AIC Lisboa 2018, Colour & Human Comfort Proceedings, p. 769.

28 **Jonauskaite, D./Abu-Akel, A./Dael, N., et al. (2020):** *Universal Patterns in Color-Emotion Associations Are Further Shaped by Linguistic and Geographic Proximity,* Psychological Science, No. 31(10), pp. 1245-1260, doi:10.1177/0956797620948810.

29 **Buether, Axel (2020):** *Die geheimnisvolle Macht der Farben. Wie sie unser Verhalten und Empfinden beeinflussen.*

30 **Several regions like Subsaharan Africa** cannot be included here, because scientifically reliable sources are hard to get a hold of.

31 **Müller, Stefan (2020):** *Interkulturelles Marketing,* p. 239.

32 **Sandikci, Ö./Rice, G. (2013):** *Handbook of Islamic Marketing,* p. 121.

33 **Schindler, Verena M. (2019):** *Jean-Philippe Lenclos' methodology of "The Geography of Colour": back to the origins and its international impact,* in: Proceedings of the International Colour Association (AIC) Conference 2019, Newtown, NSW, Australia, pp. 54-63.

34 **Dupey García,Élodie (2017):** *The material of color in pre-Columbian codices. Insights from cultural history,* in: Ancient Mesoamerica 28(1), pp. 21-40.

35 **Guirola, Christina (2010):** *Natural Dyes. Used in Mesoamerica since prehispanic age,* Asociacion FLAAR Mesoamerica. URL: http://www.maya-archaeology.org/FLAAR_Reports_on_Mayan_archaeology_Iconography_publications_books_articles/13_etnobothany_etnohistory_archaeology_precolumbian_mayan_civilization_natural_dye_fibers_textile_ink.pdf [23.02.2021].

36 **Based on an interview with a Roma couple** from south-east Hungary carried out by Enikö Papp on Aug. 31, 2020.

37 **URL:** https://www.deutschlandfunk.de/der-froehliche-friedhof.1242.de.html?dram:article_id=18944 [23.02.2021].

38 **Herrera-Sobek, Maria (ed.) (2012):** *Celebrating Latino Folklore. An Encyclopedia of Cultural Traditions,* Volume 1: A-D, pp. 405-407.

39 **Not specified (2012):** *Que Significa Ofrenda Muertos Elementos,* Universia México. URL: https://de.scribd.com/document/327613413/Que-Significa-Ofrenda-Muertos-Elementos [23.02.2021].

40 **Flores Farfán, José Antonio (2020):** *Yauhtli and Cempoalxochitl: The sacred marigolds. Tagetes species in Aztec medicine and religion.* URL: https://www.academia.edu/37945160/Yauhtli_and_Cempoalxochitl_The_sacred_marigolds_Tagetes_species_in_Aztec_medicine_and_religion [23.02.2021].

41 **The Gospel of Mark, 15:** pp. 16-17.

42 **Cox-Tamay, L. D./Cervantes-Uribe, Jocelyn S. (2016):** Laelias: Flores mágicas y ceremoniales, in: Desde el Herbario CICY 8, S. 122-127. URL: https://docplayer.es/22581313-Laelias-flores-magicas-y-ceremoniales.html [23.02.2021].

43 Based on e-mail correspondence with the French historian Jean-Christian Petitfils from July 12, 2020.

44 **Darmaputera, Eka (1997):** Pancasila and the Search for Identity and Modernity in Indonesian Society: A Cultural and Ethical Analysis.

45 **URL:** https://www.kompas.com/skola/read/2020/02/05/183000869/simbol-negara-garuda-pancasila [23.02.2021].

46 **Kurniawan, Machful Indra (2017):** *Pancasila as A Basis For Nation's Character Education,* in: Advances in Social Science, Education and Humanities Research (ASSHR), Nr. 125 /1st International Conference on Intellectuals' Global Responsibility (ICIGR). The five principles of Pancasila: 1. Belief in the one and only God. (Ketuhanan yang Maha Esa), 2. A just and civilized humanity. (Kemanusiaan yang Adil dan Beradab), 3. Unity of Indonesia. (Persatuan Indonesia), 4. Democracy, led by the wisdom of the representatives of the people (Kerakyatan yang Dipimpin oleh Hikmat Kebjaksanaan dalam permusyawaratan/perwakilan), 5. Social justice for all Indonesian people. (Keadilan Sosial bagi Seluruh Rakyat Indonesia).

47 **Jegalus, Norbertus (2009):** *Das Verhältnis von Politik, Religion und Zivilreligion untersucht am Beispiel der Pancasila,* Beiträge zur Politikwissenschaft, vol. 11, pp. 148 ff.

48 **"Warna kuning emas melambangkan keagungan bangsa atau keluhuran Negara."** Gesetz der Republik Indonesien, No. 24, 2009, p. 15.

49 **Tjakraningrat, Kangjeng Pangeran Harya./ R Soemodidjojo/ Siti Woerjan Soemadiyah Noeradyo (1980):** *Kitab primbon Betaljemur adammakna.*

50 **Sindhunata, Gabriel P. (2018):** *Anak Bajang Menggiring Angin,* p. 213. And Statistics for 2020 at URL: https://www.statista.com/statistics/320160/employment-by-economic-sector-in-indonesia/ [01.10.2020].

51 **Hasyim, M./Rachmawati, A. (2018):** *Bahasa Warna: Konsep Warna dalam Budaya Jawa, Semiotika,* p. 9, https://www.researchgate.net/publication/325391940_Bahasa_Warna_Konsep_Warna_dalam_Budaya_Jawa.

52 **International Conference on Maritime and Archipelago (ICoMA 2018), Nirmala Masilamani, Business Law Department, BINUS University, Jakarta, Indonesia.** This is an open access article under the CC BY-NC license. URL: http://creativecommons.org/licenses/by-nc/4.0/ [23.02.2021].

53 **Bellwood, P./ Fox, J. J./ Tryon, D. (ed.) (1995):** *The Austronesians: Historical and Comparative Perspectives.*

54 **Green, Amy M. (2005):** *Rangi above/Papa below, Tangaroa ascendant, water all around us: Austronesian creation myths,* S. 8. URL: https://digitalscholarship.unlv.edu/rtds/1938 [23.02.2021].

55 **Reid, A./Chambert-Loir, H. (ed.) (2002):** *The Potent Dead: Ancestors, saints and heroes in contemporary Indonesia.*

56 **Sukarno, Cindy Adams (2011):** *Bung Karno, Penyambung Lidah Rakyat Indonesia,* p. 272.

57 **"Warna kuning emas melambangkan keagungan bangsa atau keluhuran Negara."** Gesetz der Republik Indonesien, No. 24, 2009, p. 16.

58 **URL:** https://ppkn.unibabwi.ac.id/2020/02/13/pancasila/ [23.02.2021].

59 **Hasyim, M./Rachmawati, A. (2018):** *Bahasa Warna: Konsep Warna dalam Budaya Jawa, Semiotika,* p. 8, https://www.researchgate.net/publication/325391940_Bahasa_Warna_Konsep_Warna_dalam_Budaya_Jawa [23.02.2021].

60 **You can find numerous music videos on YouTube if you enter the search term "Pancasila".**
The song "Mars Pancasila" (1956) can be found in every school songbook. Mars refers to the tempo of the Marseillaise (1792), the French national anthem, which is associated in Indonesia with the desire for independence. It was forbidden to sing the Marseillaise under Dutch colonial rule. Today, like the symbol, the song is called "Garuda Pancasila". There is no rigidly prescribed interpretation of Pancasila and it has also changed under millennials.
A new version of the popular folk song "Garuda di Dadaku" (Garuda in my heart) was produced by the alternative rock band Netral 2009 for the soundtrack of the film of the same name. Nachfolgend der Songtext von "Garuda di Dadaku" auf Englisch:
Garuda in my heart *Come on, sons o the nation / Give pride to the nation / Make us proud / Indonesia*
Show the world / I the Motherland / Worthy to be champions / Indonesia
Long live my country / Beloved homeland /Great Indonesia / Long live my country / Beloved homeland / Great Indonesia
Garuda on my heart / Garuda is my pride / I'm sure today will definitely win ... / Kindle your spirits / Show your sportsmanship / I'm sure
today will definitely win ...
Garuda on my heart / Garuda is my pride / I'm sure today will definitely win ... / Kindle your spirits / Show your sportsmanship / I'm sure
today will definitely win ...

CHAPTER 5 | INTERCULTURAL EXPERTISE

1   **Meyer, E. (2014):** *The Culture Map: Decoding How People Think, Lead, and Get Things Done Across Cultures,* Kindle version, p. 171.

2   **ibid,.** p. 247

3   **"They give the pupils something to do, not something to learn; and the doing is of such a nature as to demand thinking, or the intentional noting of connections; learning naturally results."** Dewey, John (1916): *Democracy and Education,* Position: 2469.

4   **Klafki, Wolfgang (2002):** *Schultheorie, Schulforschung und Schulentwicklung im politisch-gesellschaftlichen Kontext,* pp. 176-195.

5   **Auernheimer, Georg (2012):** *Einführung in die interkulturelle Pädagogik,* p. 59.

6   **Intermedia Arts and Creative Technology - Volume 1:** CREATIVEARTS, S. 147-155. doi:10.5220/0009032101470155.

7   **Diah Mayang Sari, Interview at University of Applied Sciences Ulm, Germany, 2015.** URL: https://workshop.intercultural.design/TiM2015/video.html [23.02.2021].

8   **Radtke, Susanne (2019):** *Educational Animations in Inter- and Monocultural Design Workshops,* in: Proceedings of the 1st International Conference on Intermedia Arts and Creative Technology - Volume 1: CREATIVEARTS, S. 147-155. doi: 10.5220/0009032101470155.

9   **Elsen, Hilke (2020):** *Gender - Sprache - Stereotype,* p. 104.

10 **Jonas, K./Schmid Mast, M. (2007):** *Stereotyp und Vorurteil,* p. 1.

11 **Allport, Gordon (1954):** *The nature of prejudice,* pp. 276-279.

12 **Radtke, Susanne P. (2016):** *Internationalisierung der Medienausbildung. Methoden und Ergebnisse am Beispiel von interkulturellen Design-Workshops in den USA, Ägypten und Indonesien,* in: Klaffke,H./Knutzen, S./Buether, A./Toscano, B. (ed.): Tagungsband Medienberufe auf neuen Wegen. Wandel der Gesellschaft, der Berufe und der dualen Ausbildung?, Technische Universität Hamburg-Harburg, Technische Bildung und Hochschuldidaktik G-3, p. 162.

13 **Lewandowska, A./Mieder, W. (ed.) (2008):** *Sprichwort-Gebrauch heute. Ein interkulturell-kontrastiver Vergleich von Sprichwörtern anhand polnischer und deutscher Printmedien,* Sprichwortforschung Bd. 26., p. 132.

14 **URL:** https://textmessage.pja.edu.pl, URL: http://design.pja.edu.pl/workshops [23.02.2021].

15 **An 'Objet trouvé' (French for 'found object')** is an everyday or natural object that becomes a work of art because an artist attributes it with aesthetic value and transforms or integrates it into their work. The term became popular at the beginning of the 20th century when many artists, like the Surrealists for example, questioned traditional ideas about the true nature of art in the sense of "every object can be a work of art."

16 **Understanding, by the way, is a fixed term used in English-language qualitative social research and is not translated. Patton defines 'understanding' as follows: "Meaningful understanding, the capacity to see things from another's perspective"** (Patton 2015, p. 56, footnote 19).

17 **In qualitative social research** in particular, there are different theoretical approaches towards our perception of reality, and how societies and the individuals populating them influence this or shape it –that is, what things they attribute what meaning to. As such, Symbolic Interactionism assumes that interactions are communicated via symbolic codifications and are based on certain conventionalized forms of interaction, gestures and rituals (cf. Kruse 2014, p. 29, footnote 21). Social Constructivism also assumes that there are no objective realities, believing instead that these are social constructs (cf. Flick 2013, p. 151, footnote 21).

18 **Geertz, Clifford (1999):** *Dichte Beschreibung. Beiträge zum Verstehen kultureller Systeme.*

19 **Patton, M. Q. (2015):** *Qualitative Research & Evaluation Method*s. 4th Edition.

20 **Meyer, Erin (2015):** *The Culture Map. Decoding How People Think, Lead, And Get Things Done Across Cultures.*

21 **Further literature: Flick, Uwe (2013):** *Konstruktivismus.* In: Flick, U./von Kardoff, E./Steinke, I. (Hrsg.): Qualitative Forschung. Ein Handbuch. 10. Aufl., S. 150-164. / **Kruse, Jan (2014):** *Qualitative Interviewforschung. Ein integrativer Ansatz.*

CHAPTER 6 | LOCAL VS. GLOBAL

1   **URL:** https://www.onlineprinters.de/magazin/die-geschichte-des-plakats/ [23.02.2021].

2   **Villaverde, Héctor (2009):** *Testimonios del diseño gráfico cubano.* 1959-1974.

3   **Valdés, Reyna María (1991):** *Cuba en la gráfica.*

4   **Fernández, Lucila (2014):** *Una isla de diseño Cuba 1960 al 2000,* Arte cubano No. 2, pp. 64-67.

5   **URL:** https://www.smashingmagazine.com/2010/01/the-legacy-of-polish-poster-design/ [23.02.2021].

6   **Rudzinski, Piotr (2009):** *Pierwsze polwiecze polskiego plakatu 1900-1950.*

7   **URL:** https://www.porta-polonica.de/de/atlas-der-erinnerungsorte/polnische-plakatkunst-der-bundesrepub-lik-der-nachkriegszeit. [23.02.2021].

8   **Eckstein, Hans (1962):** *Vorwort in: Plakate aus Polen* (Ausst.kat.), München, Die Neue Sammlung.

9   **URL:** https://www.smb.museum/ausstellungen/detail/der-salon-der-plakate-ist-die-strasse-die-schule-der-polni-schen-plakatkunst-1950-1970/ [23.02.2021].

10 **URL:** https://www.europa.clio-online.de/essay/id/fdae-1656 [23.02.2021].

11 **URL:** https://www.sueddeutsche.de/leben/lichtbilder-ganz-kleines-kino-1.3223598 [23.02.2021].

12 **URL:** https://hgdi.wordpress.com/2009/05/19/timeline-for-indonesian-graphic-design-history/ [23.02.2021].

13 **Brattinga, Maartje (2014):** *Advertising in the Dutch East Indies. In search of a tropical style,* in: Wimba. Jurnal Komunikasi Visual & Multimedia, Vol. 6, No. 2, pp. 3-4.

14 **URL:** https://hgdi.wordpress.com/2009/05/03/1900s/ [23.02.2021].

15 **URL:** https://de.statista.com/statistik/daten/studie/253272/umfrage/alphabetisierung-in-indonesien/ and https://datatopics.worldbank.org/world-development-indicators/themes/people.html [23.02.2021].

16 **URL:** http://www.adgi.or.id/en/about [23.02.2021].

17 **Sumarijanto, Lucia C. (2007):** *In Search of a Style. The Issue of Cultural Identity and Graphic Design in Indonesia.* Thesis for the degree of Master Science (Communication Design) at Pratt Institute School of Art and Design, December 2003, pp. 33-49.

18 **John Kudos,** email correspondence from Feb. 2, 2021.

19 **Wulan, R. R. (2017):** *The Myth of White Skin. A Postcolonial Review of Cosmetics Ads in Indonesia,* in: SHS Web of Conferences 33, doi: 10.1051.

20 **URL:** https://smoking-room.net/pria-punya-selera-gudang-garam-international/ [23.02.2021].

21 **s. footnote 1: URL:** https://hgdi.wordpress.com/2009/05/19/timeline-for-indonesian-graphic-design-history/ [23.02.2021].

PICTURE CREDITS

1.01 Ilustration: Jan Büttner
1.02 Ilustration: I Kadek Buda Patrayasa
1.03 Photo: Susanne P. Radtke
1.04-1.06 Illustration: Beryl Natalie Janssenn
1.08 Concept/Illustration: Mimi Rehmann
1.09 Illustration: Beryl Natalie Janssen
1.11 1908: (https://commons.wikimedia.org/wiki/File:Tube_map_1908-2.jpg), "Tube map 1908-2", edited, https://creativecommons.org/publicdomain/zero/1.0/legalcode
1933: https://en.wikipedia.org/wiki/Harry_Beck#/media/File:Beck_Map_1933.jpg
1.12 Piet Mondrian artist QS:P170,Q151803 (https://commons.wikimedia.org/wiki/File:Blossoming_apple_tree,_by_Piet_Mondriaan.jpg)
Piet Mondrian artist QS:P170,Q151803 (https://commons.wikimedia.org/wiki/File:-Mondriaan_-_No._11.jpg), "Mondriaan - No. 11"
Piet Mondrian artist QS:P170,Q151803 (https://commons.wikimedia.org/wiki/File:Piet_Mondriaan,_1921_-_Composition_en_rouge,_jaune,_bleu_et_noir.jpg)
1.13 Illustration: Beryl Natalie Janssen
1.14 Germany East (c. 1969), Germany regional e.g. Dresden / Saxony (1996) and after 1989 in part for Germany West
1.15 1. Germany (pedestrian pair spec. Frankfurt am Main/Hessia, Denmark (spec. Fredericia), 2. Germany (spec. Rhineland-Palatinate)
1.16 Austria (Innsbruck, temporary for winter half year)
1.17 Mustienes, C./Hilland, T. (2006): Icons. Colors Signs.
Taschen (ed.) (2009): COLORS. 1000 Signs.
NB.: German Reich 1939: same sign as in Federal Republic of Germany, (1949–1953), German Democratic Republic (1949–1956) and Netherlands 1941
1.18-1.21 l. to r.
RHOMBUS: Verena Seitz, Ashely Cooper, Verena Seitz, https://pixabay.com/de/stra%C3%9Fenschild-warnung-b%C3%A4r-gefahr-2630485, Ashely Cooper, Verena Seitz, Susanne P. Radtke, Hubert Mousseigne, Verena Seitz, Verena Seitz
TRIANGLE: Hal Brinkley, https://pixabay.com/de/photos/warnschild-verkehrs-schild-schild-2446886, Susanne P. Radtke, Roly Vasquez, Lariset Aguilar, https://amp.spb.kp.ru/daily/26589.5/3604756, Lewis Nightingale, Mira Wagner, https://www.zoonar.de/photo/strassenschild-warnt-vor-wandernden-sanddnen-oman_2664129.html, Joachim Kant
CIRCLE: Ashely Cooper, Verena Seitz, Verena Seitz
Verena Seitz, Verena Seitz, Verena Seitz, Verena Seitz, Diego Catto, Verena Seitz, Olaf Hoffmann
SPECIAL SHAPES: Olaf Hoffmann, Carsten Lange, Anita Diepold, Dinna Louise C. Dayao, Ashely Cooper, Sebastian Volkholz, Greg Montani, Susanne P. Radtke, Verena Seitz, Sebastian Volkholz
1.22-1.25 Design: Yossi Lemel
2.01-2.02 Ilustration: Jan Büttner
2.04 Illustration: Susanne P. Radtke
2.05 Illustration: Bachelor thesis Niko Winkler, 2019
2.06-2.15 Illustration: Susanne P. Radtke
2.16 Students' works l. to r.: Jan Herok, Jasdev Bhogal, Felix Dedek, Jennifer Beifuss
2.18 Wassily Kandinsky, "Dance Curves: On the Dances of Palucca" Das Kunstblatt, Potsdam, vol. 10, no. 3 (1926), pp. 117-21
2.19-2.22 Student work: Jan Büttner
2.23 Illustration: Susanne P. Radtke
2.24 Illustration: I Kadek Buda Patrayasa
2.25 Photo: Verena Seitz
2.26 Photo: Wolfgang Siol; HfG Archive / Museum Ulm, Inv. No. 61.0324
2.27 Designer: Rob Janoff, 1977
2.28 Designer: Anton Stankowski, 1974
2.29 Photos: Background: Lars-Thore Rehbach
top to bottom: Lars-Thore Rehbach, Lars-Thore Rehbach, Thomas Kärcher
2.30 Student work: Li Hang
2.31 Students' works, l. to r. Marie-Sophie Stelte, Erdem Demet and Angelique Gelhar, Philipp Kühlein, Andreas Bindseil and David Cisar
3.01 Graphic: Paul Daniel
3.02 Adapted by Fay, Nicolas/Ellison, T. Mark (2014): Iconicity: From Sign to System in Human Communication and Language, DOI: 10.1075/pc.22.2.05fay, p. 245
3.03 Graphics: Paul Daniel
3.04-3.06 Illustration: Angela Ziegler
3.08 Illustration: Jan Büttner

3.09 Student work: Jan Büttner
3.10 Student work, top: Jenny Beuth, bottom: Andreas Rusch
3.11 Illustration: Franziska Wagner
3.12 Ilustrations: I Kadek Buda Patrayasa, Paul Daniel
3.13 Model: Wulf Architekten, Stuttgart, Germany
3.14-3.16 Design: Saki Mafundikwa
3.17 Design: Anushka Sani
3.18 Design: Thaakierah Abdul
3.19-3.21 Design: Marian Bantjes
3.22 Design: Elizabeth Resnick,
3.23-3.24 Design: Gustavo Greco
3.25 Susana Machicao,
3.26-3.27 Design: Georgios D. Matthiopoulos
3.28-3.30 Design: Typical organization: Joshua Olsthoorn and Kostas Vlachakis
3.31 Design: k2design
3.32-3.33 Design: Katerina Antonaki
3.3-3.35 Design: MNP
3.36-3.49 Sources: Zhiqian Li
3.50 Design: Yi Meng Wu
3.51 Design: Hong Jie Guan
3.52 Design: Yan Song Li
3.53 Design: Hai Long Xiang
3.54-3.56 Sources: Haytham Nawar
3.57-3.58 Design: Muhammad Yaqoob, 1834
3.59 Source: Haytham Nawar
3.60 Design: Pascal Zoghbi for the Eye Magazine #90, 2015
3.61 Source: Haytham Nawar
3.62-3.63 Design: Golnar Kat Rahmani
3.64-3.65 Design: Nada Abdallah
3.66-3.68 Design: Engy Aly
3.69-3.70 Design: Yosra Gamal, Mirna Noaman & Nada Hesham, Yasser Nazmy, Ahmed Hammoud
4.01 Bachelor thesis: Joshua Schlaier
4.02-4.03 Illustration: Paul Daniel
4.04 Painting: Wen Shu (https://commons.wikimedia.org/wiki/File:%E6%96%87%E4%BF%B6_%E3%80%8A%E8%8A%B1%E9%B8%9F%E5%9B%BE%E3%80%8B.jpg)
4.05 AKG935663_Newton's experiment with fracturing light,
Graphic credit: akg / Science Photo Library
4.06-4.08 Illustration: Paul Daniel
4.09 Design: Susanne P. Radtke
4.10 Photo: unknown
4.11 Student works, l. to r.: Franziska Emhardt, all others from Martina Stoll
4.12 Illustration: Beryl Natalie Janssen
4.13 Student work: Max Willier
4.14 Student work: Simon Deering
4.15 Illustration: Jan Büttner
4.16 Foto: Thomas Kärcher
4.17 First Santa Claus designed by cartoonist and graphic designer Haddon Sundblom for Cola-Cola in 1931.
4.18 (https://commons.wikimedia.org/wiki/File:Empress_Catherine_The_Great_1787_(Mikhail_Shibanov).JPG), "Empress Catherine The Great 1787 (Mikhail Shibanov)"
4.19 Rembrandt artist QS:P170,Q5598 (https://commons.wikimedia.org/wiki/File:Rembrandt_-_De_Staalmeesters-_het_college_van_staalmeesters_(waardijns)_van_het_Amsterdamse_lakenbereidersgilde_-_Google_Art_Project.jpg), "Rembrandt - De Staalmeesters- het college van staalmeesters (waardijns) van het Amsterdamse lakenbereidersgilde - Google Art Project"
4.20 Illustration: Beryl Natalie Janssen
4.21 Jonauskaite, D., Abu-Akel, A., Dael, N., Oberfeld, D., Abdel-Khalek, A. M., Al-Rasheed, A. S., Antonietti, J.-P., Bogushevskaya, V., Chamseddine, A., Chkonia, E., Corona, V., Fonseca-Pedrero, E., Griber, Y. A., Grimshaw, G., Hasan, A. A., Havelka, J., Hirnstein, M., Karlsson, B. S. A., Laurent, E., ... Mohr, C. (2020). Universal Patterns in Color-Emotion Associations Are Further Shaped by Linguistic and Geographic Proximity. Psychological Science, 31(10), 1245–1260. https://doi.org/10.1177/0956797620948810, Abb. 3, S. 7

4.22 With the kind permission of Lenclos, Jean-Philippe (1995): Les couleurs de l'Europe. géographie de la couleur, p. 123
4.23 Graphic: Paul Daniel
4.24-4.26 Design: Ghada Wali
4.27-4.28 Design: Hanny Kardinata
4.29-4.32 Design: Shino Suefusa
4.33 Design: Eduardo Barrera Arambarri
4.34 Design: Leo Lin
4.35 Design: Sophia Shih
4.36 Design: O'Plerou Grebet
4.37 Design: Lulu Zhao,
4.38 Design: Ping Mu
4.39 Design: Jing Yang
4.40 Design: Jing Xiao
4.41 Illustration: Beryl Natalie Janssen, Alexandra Stoll
4.42 Illustration: Paul Daniel
4.43 https://pixabay.com/de/users/andyg-144138/
4.44 Foto: Filiberto Santillan
4.45 Photo: Alice Triquet
4.46-4.47 Bachelor thesis: Robin Muster
4.48 Photo: Susanne P. Radtke
4.49 Photo: https://de.depositphotos.com/stock-photos/tumpeng.html?filter=all&-qview=271353866
4.52 Illustration: Jan Büttner
4.53 Photo: Katrin Hinz
4.54 Graphic: Katrin Hinz
4.55 Illustration: Antonia Mahlke
4.56 Pictograms: Lisa Voigt
4.57 Photo: Katrin Hinz
4.58 Photo: Katrin Hinz
Literature for the graphics
4.20 Color semantics of the religions
4.23 Cultural spaces and their color interpretations
Aslam, Mubeen M. (2006): Are You Selling the Right Colour? A Cross-cultural Review of Colour as a Marketing Cue Journal of Marketing Communications, Vol. 12, No. 1, S. 15–30.
Blum, Lothar B. (2010): Colours & Cultures, Beiträge zur empirischen Designfor-schung, URL: https://designforschung.wordpress.com/2010/05/20/colours-cultures/.
Buether, Axel (2020): Die geheimnisvolle Macht der Farben: Wie sie unser Verhalten und Empfinden beeinflussen, Kindle Version (German Edition).
Chase, Emily (2014-2015): Colors of Judaism, in: DERECH HATEVA. A Journal of Torah and Science. A Publication of Stern College for Women, Yeshiva University, Vol. 19.
De Bortoli, Mario & Maroto, Jesús (2008): Colours Across Cultures: Translating Co-lours in Interactive Marketing Communications, Global Propaganda, Granada, Spain, URL: http://www.globalpropaganda.fresa.net/articles/TranslatingColours.pdf.
Dieckmann-von Bünau, Detlef (2008): Farben (AT), Scientific Bible Lexicon in the In-ternet, URL: https://www.bibelwissenschaft.de/wibilex/das-bibellexikon/lexikon/sachwort/anzeigen/details/farben-at/ch/b43afcce7c87584a7111d922a4f3ac61/.
Fauzan bin Abu Bakar, Muhammad (2015): Colours of Islam, Academia.edu, URL: https://www.academia.edu/6434115/Colours_of_Islam.
Halbgebauer, Nora (2008): Polychromie romanischer Portale in Wien und Niederös-terreich, degree thesis, University of Vienna, History-Cultural Sciences Faculty, URL: http://othes.univie.ac.at/974/1/2008-08-26_9400017.pdf.
Jonauskaite, D. et al. (2020): Universal Patterns in Color-Emotion Associations Are Further Shaped by Linguistic and Geographic Proximity, Psychological Science, 31(10), pp. 1245–1260, doi:10.1177/0956797620948810.
Li, Yuhai: On the Symbolic Meaning of Color Words in Chines Traditional Culture (chin.), URL: https://m.xzbu.com/1/view-6162666.htm [16.02.2021].
Morton, Jill (2004): Global Color Clues and Taboos, PDF document published by COLORCOM®.
Namiri, Mahsa Esmaeili (2017): Symbolic Meaning of Colors in Traditional Mosques, Submitted to the Institute of Graduate Studies and Research in partial fulfillment of the requirements for the degree of Master of Science in Architecture, Eastern Mediterranean University, Gazimağusa, North Cyprus, URL: http://i-rep.emu.edu.tr:8080/xmlui/handle/11129/4314.
Panja, Ishita (2020): Color in Architecture, Department of Architecture, B. Arch. Dissertation, ITM School of Architecture & Town planning, N.H.-24, Bakshi KaTalab, Lucknow, Uttar Pradesh, URL: https://issuu.com/rediffmail9741/docs/colour__in_architecture__ishita_panja_

Shirgaonkar, Varsha (2017): Colors ans Color Symbolism in Ancient Buddhism and Hinduism: Reflections in Art and Rituals, Department of History, S.N.D.T. Women's University, Mumbai 400020. URL: https://www.academia.edu/35893126/COLOURS_AND_COLOUR_SYMBOLISM_IN_ANCIENT_BUDDHISM_AND_HINDUISM_REFLEC-TIONS_IN_ART_AND_RITUALS.
5.01 Clockwise:
Student animation: Blasius Vebiyona Abi, Ade Surya Nanda, Dharmawan Arif Setiawan, Niklas Luther, Adrian Jehne, Rebekka Egl
Student animation: Leony Agustine, Tiara Alifa Putri, Jenny Beifuss, Markus Leukel, Marina Masud Mizoguchi, Melina Reich
Photo: Susanne P. Radtke
Photo: James Wasswa, Uganda
Photo: Susanne P. Radtke
Photo: Susanne P. Radtke
Photo: Agnieszka Ziemiszewska, Polen
Middle:
Student animation: Maira Bizimi, Jan Herok, Nathalie Hochholzer, Ioannis Katsibras
5.02 Graphic: Angela Ziegler
5.03 Student works: Jan Gurbandt, Maximilian Maier
5.04 Student works: A. Braun, H. Guillford, R. Carlyle, M. Maier, S. Tan
5.05 Photo unknown
5.06 Student works: Franziska Wegmann, Sophie Griebel, Irna Audina, Bayu Santoso
5.07 Student works: Khansa Dewi K, Arjuna Kresna W, Kristina Schirmer, Sebastian Volkholz
5.08 Graphic: Frank Rausch
5.09 Photo: Susanne P. Radtke
5.10 Student works: Jonathan Bail, Lena Heger, Nathalie Hochholzer, Bayu Santosa, Kristina Schirmer,
Sebastian Volkholz
5.11 Student works, Egyptian students: Hoda Abd El Latif, Mona Diab, Emma El Benany, Heba El Kest,
Iman El Shenawy, Salma El Ashkar, Sandra Fahim Botros,
Nawarra Hany Mehrem, Ayah O Moustafa, Kanzy Taha, deutsche Studierende:
Ulrike Grau, Andrea Jall, Bernd Kächler, Diana Macuta, Robert Martinez,
Andrea Prade, Moritz Schwindt, Nadja Weber, Maximilian Willier,
Anastaszija Zelic
5.12 Student works: Judith Bahr, Xenia Engelke, Maxi Stumpp, Regina Sembiring, Yannis Katsimpras
5.13 Photo: Susanne P. Radtke
5.14 Student works: Maira Bizimi, Jan Herok, Nathalie Hochholzer, Ioannis Katsibras
5.15 Student works: Lydia Papaconstantinou, Joshua Schlaier, Samantha Schraag
5.16 Student works: Jan Büttner, Karolin Knapik, Zoi Panteliadou, Evanthia Papa-kosma
5.17 Photo: unknown
5.19 Student works: Emmerich Buchmüller, Anna Krutova, Mackenzie Moran, Stephanie Reiner
5.20 Student works: Jennifer Cheung, Saskia Müller, Kenta Naoi, Christopher Wilutzki
5.21-5.22 Design: Lu Yu
5.23 Photo: Celine Benachour
5.24-5.25 Illustration: Blasius Vebiyona Abi, Ade Surya Nanda, Dharmawan Arif Setiawan
5.26 BZ: Illustration: Jennifer Steffen
5.27-5.30 Design: Rayan Abdullah
5.31 Photo: Sebastian Volkholz
5.32 Graphic: Angela Ziegler
5.34 Sources: Agnieszka Ziemiszewska
5.35 Photo: Sigrid A. Bathke
6.01 Illustration: Angela Ziegler
6.02-6.03 Design: Edel Rodríguez Mola
6.04-6.07 Design: Indania del Río
6.08-6.09 Design: Agnieszka Ziemiszewska
6.10-6.13 Design: Jerzy Skakun and Joanna Górska,
6.14-6.18 Design: Marcin Władyka
6.19 Design. John Kudos
6.20-6.21 Design: Studio Batu
6.22-6.23 Design: Indieguerillas
6.23-6.27 Design: Henri Kusbiantoro

NOTES

This QR code leads to
www.intercultural-design-basics.com

↗ Enter the code on the sticker on the front flap.
   You will receive your personalized Google Play Store
   or Apple's App Store promo code.
↗ Now unlock the app "Intercultural Design Basics" using
   your promo code.
↗ Point the camera of your smartphone or tablet at the
   QR codes inside the book and off you go!

The following content is available on the app:

▶️   Videos (interviews with designers, workshops and animations)

📦   Projections in augmented reality (visual input in 3D space)

🗔   Galleries and slideshows (learning – step by step)

🎮   Games (learning by doing)

Have fun!